**DO NOT REMOVE
CARDS FROM POCKET**

THE TERRY LECTURES

# Constantine and Religious Liberty

# Constantine and
# Religious Liberty

## by Hermann Doerries

UNIVERSITY OF GÖTTINGEN

TRANSLATED FROM THE GERMAN
## by Roland H. Bainton

YALE UNIVERSITY DIVINITY SCHOOL

New Haven: YALE UNIVERSITY PRESS 1960

# 𝔓reface

I INVITE YOU to accompany me on a journey to the remote past, not to stimulate antiquarian interest, but to recover for the benefit of the present a segment of a lost age. History has been regarded as prophecy in reverse, for whereas prophecy visualizes the future, history revives the past after the manner of that seer of the Old Testament who, looking upon a field of bleached bones, saw them resume life when breathed upon by the Spirit of God (Ezek. 37). To bring the past is worth a laborious quest.

The process is comparatively simple when we are dealing with the history of the earth. The stone witnesses of past aeons tell only one story of the world around them and of the nature and conditions of life in their time. The case is quite different when we deal with human history, for which the records are not rocks but books, for sometimes the books are of a quality surpassing anything in our own time, constituting a portion of our spiritual heritage, and so requiring to be appropriated afresh for each new age. The historian then becomes, as it were, an ambassador of his own time to remote periods, a pioneer exploring El Dorados of the past.

The purpose of the Terry lectures includes this commission to reinterpret, and determines the spirit in which the lecturer approaches his task. The moment has come now for me to make a responsible report on the results of my own trek. For although the historian, while immersed in his journey of research, is not able to think often of his own home and time—since he has to do justice to that strange country he seeks to know —he is bound to his own time by the very manner in which he views the past. Every generation selects its own vista, fastens upon that which has lain hitherto unnoticed, and is no longer interested in that over which the preceding generation displayed enthusiasm. In this way every generation stands in a new relation to what has gone before. Only the ascertainment of facts has an uninterrupted course. Here we stand upon the work of our predecessors.

However much the historian may be susceptible to the changes and the requirements of his own time, he must not allow his presuppositions to determine what happened in the past, or be hasty in imposing his questions or his answers upon the material he is investigating. In the end, history will take him by the hand and lead him to her truth. But if we were not to pose questions of value, if we were not to inquire wherein scholarship serves life, our labor would be vain. If not at the beginning, then certainly at the end, all historical work must confront the questions to which we now address ourselves. Even from the most remote eras a voice must reach us and a word become audible which we can regard as addressed to ourselves.

Constantine and religious liberty—this, our theme, does not have reference to a stage in the process whereby in the modern world religious liberty was fought for, apparently won, and then universally threatened. The history of modern tolerance scarcely begins before the sixteenth century and in its most active form hardly before the eighteenth and even nineteenth, when we began to enjoy the fruits of the long struggle. Of course, Constantine's tolerance is closer to us than, say, Asoka's in India. But just as an expert on India might present the religious liberty accorded by this ruler as a significant chapter in Indian history, so shall we present that of Constantine as an important moment in the history of late antiquity. Perhaps, as we are so engaged and without any attempt on our part to trace connections, the facts themselves may speak to us.

Thanks are due the Terry Foundation Committee for the friendly invitation extended to me to deliver these lectures. It is an honor to come to Yale; and to focus my special field, the Church History of the fourth century, on the question of religious liberty is suggested by the very *genius loci*. Liberty found her place in Yale and some remarkable books concerning it came forth from here.

I am grateful also for the critical and editorial assistance rendered me by Ernst Berneburg and Udo Schulze.

To Roland H. Bainton, the scholarly friend whose research brought so much light to the intricate history of this movement, I am very deeply indebted. His translation of my lectures is more than a mere transmission of words; often it has made for greater clarity: many a train of thought has been tightened, many a sentence is now more terse. Mrs. Bainton was a patient instructor in the oral delivery of a language to which I came late in life. While reading the manuscript for the printer, the chapel of the Yale Divinity School arose before my eyes once more, renewing my gratitude for the kindly reception accorded lectures and lecturer. At the same time it made the more lively a feeling of uneasiness as well as joy: uneasiness over the fact that previous supports of religious liberty now seem uncertain not only in a Europe shaken to its foundations but even in the new world; joy that it is a common task, here and there, to establish them more firmly. The historical reflections presented in these lectures are designed to assist in the realization of this task.

The printed text affects its author differently from the manuscript. It prompts him to renewed reflection on what he has said and to elaboration of that to which he has merely alluded. I would like to have followed up further the Roman rejection of the Christian desire for tolerance; I wanted to show why a restoration not only elevates the essence of the old into consciousness

viii

but gently remolds it in the process. Furthermore, I wanted to discuss in detail some of the latest investigations, for example of the cult of the emperors. But pressing duties have prevented the realization of such desires.

It only remains for me to express gratitude to David Horue, my editor, and to the Yale University Press for granting me a visitor's privilege in their midst, thereby keeping alive something of the feeling of home that binds me to Yale.

H. D.

*Göttingen*
*May 1960*

# Contents

# 1. Constantine and the Heathen

PRIOR to Constantine, the spokesmen of the persecuted Christian Church were continually demanding
freedom at the hands of the Roman emperors. The
grounds advanced were varied. The defenders of the
faith, the so-called Apologists of the second century,
who addressed pleas to the emperors pointed to the
advantage that would accrue to the empire by reason
of such tolerance, but when they claimed to be law-
abiding, orderly citizens,[1] the retort lay easily to hand
that they were breaking the law and disturbing public
order. They offered themselves to the emperor as
reliable confederates in his efforts against innovation
and insurrection, but those were precisely the offenses
with which they were charged. Their fight against the
legions of demons could not very well be regarded
with favor by the rulers of the state, because these
very demons were none other than the gods revered
since time immemorial.

The contention of the Christian theologians cut
deeper when they sought to discover a causal connection between the coincident rise of the Roman empire
and the Christian religion, for was not Christ born

1. Justin Martyr, *Apology* 1.3.

1

during the census instituted by the first emperor Augustus?[2] But so bold a pretention could not well expect to find credence among pagan hearers.

The misgivings of the government were hardly resolved when the faith that demanded tolerance was known to hold aloof not only from the temple but also from the forum and the military camp, and the spiritual support that Origen promised to the imperial forces[3] was not deemed a satisfactory substitute for the military service that was renounced, if not by all at least by many of the Christians. Moreover, if at first there was little disposition to invite Christians to serve as magistrates and judges, the readiness of the state to make the offer did not exceed the willingness of the Christians to accept it. They abstained from public life by deliberate choice, and not merely because they were excluded.

Yet among all the Christian writers it was the most aloof—Tertullian, keen and sarcastic—who found for Christian freedom the formula most tenable by reason of its precision and universality. He threw back the charge of irreligion made against the Christians and charged those who made it with subversion of religion through the restrictions they placed upon its freedom. "As no man loves insincere service, even less does God," said he.[4] This assertion, by grounding religion

2. Cf. Melito of Sardis (Eusebius, *Historia Ecclesiasticus* 4.26.7–11).

3. *Contra celsum* 8.73.

4. Tertullian, *Apologeticum* 24.6: Videte enim, ne et hoc ad

in sincere personal conviction, undercut the connection between religion and the state characteristic of antiquity. "The religion of one man neither hurts nor helps another," continued Tertullian. The considerations here adduced acquired a philosophical character as deductions, though mainly negative, from the very essence of religion as from a universal idea. Again: "No one can be compelled to worship against his will." This makes religion a matter of inner persuasion, not only for Christianity but also for the performance of pagan sacrifice. For, said Tertullian, "even sacrifice calls for willingness."

These universal propositions were applied to the immediate situation. "If you force us to sacrifice, you will not thereby benefit your gods. They will not be pleased by a resentful offering unless they are addicted to strife, and one addicted to strife is no god." The attentive hearer could observe a new tone here, and particularly in the phrase often to be quoted: "It is not proper to religion to compel religion." We do not know precisely what this meant for Tertullian; the

inreligiositatis elogium concurrat, adimere libertatem religionis et interdicere optionem divinitatis, ut non liceat mihi colere quem velim, sed cogar colere quem nolim. Nemo se ab invito coli volet, ne homo quidem. *Ad Scapulam* 2.2: Humani iuris et naturalis potestatis est unicuique, quod putaverit, colere nec alii obest aut prodest alterius religio. Sed nec religionis est cogere religionem, quae sponte suscipi debeat, non vi, cum et hostiae ab animo libenti expostulentur. Ita etsi nos compuleritis ad sacrificandum, nihil praestabitis diis vestris; ab invitis enim sacrificia non desiderabunt, nisi si contentiosi sunt; contentiosus autem deus non est.

statement bears various interpretations. Our task is to consider by whom and under what circumstances it was spoken. At the time, it was an expression of a faith under pressure to participate in the sacrifices of the imperial cult, a faith that sought to persuade the persecutor to remove this pressure. Another African theologian, Lactantius, a century later, taking up again the note struck by Tertullian, that no one can be compelled to worship against his will, affirmed that "there is nothing which so depends on free will as religion." [5] Have we here an expression of Stoic freedom from all circumstance, or an expression of the Christian freedom of faith? "In freedom alone," said Lactantius, "religion has its fortress." [6] This phrase also had reverberations, and despite divergent interpretations was not devoid of a hearing. In its own context it carried intense conviction in a time of severe persecution— the expression of an oppressed and undaunted faith.

A persecuted minority craved relief and did so in the name of a universal principle to which anyone could appeal. To us this principle appears incontestable (though the history of our own times shows that it is still not universally accepted), but in that day it was not among the self-evident truths. In antiquity none assumed that religion rests on free decisions, which each must make for himself: this could have been true only if a man's course were in a measure dissociated from the religious and social order in which

5. *Divinae institutiones* 5.19.11, 23.
6. *Epitome* 49.1, 2.

4

he found himself. The degree to which Christians did dissociate themselves from this order made of them a minority.

The Christian plea for tolerance, therefore, in spite of historical, philosophical, and religious arguments, received at that time no hearing.

Not merely the "bad" emperors refused to listen, but also the noblest. The prohibition had nothing to do with the magnanimity or enmity of particular rulers. "Every people has its religion," said Cicero, "and we have ours." [7] This persuasion enabled the Romans to allow conquered peoples to retain their own religions: the Romans were obligated to serve the Roman gods, but not, to the same degree, the Syrians and Egyptians. And whereas the Romans attempted at first to restrict the alien cults to the lands where they were indigenous, at the same time no serious impediment was offered their dissemination, and soon the Romans themselves, increasingly, were becoming initiates. When in the beginning of the third century Roman citizenship was conferred upon all free inhabitants of the empire, all restrictions on religion were removed. In Rome the cult of the Syrian sun god and the Egyptian Isis so far flourished that the former received recognition for the birthday of the sun god on the 25th of December as the official religious holiday,[1]

7. *Pro Flacco* 28: Sua cuique civitati religio est, nostra nobis.
1. Cf. Hermann Karl Usener, "Das Weihnachtsfest," *Religionsgeschichtliche Untersuchungen, 1* Bonn, 1899. Louis M. O. Duchesne, *Christian Worship,* London, 1903.

whereas the latter became in the fourth century the focus for the opposition among the Roman aristocracy to the spread of Christianity. The coins struck and widely distributed by the senate, the so-called *contorniati*, bore the image of the ship of Isis to offset the Christian symbols on the official coinage.

Of course the freedom of the oriental cults meant that now all Romans could be required with even greater insistence to perform official religious duties, but this was no fundamental innovation. From the outset compliance with the imperial cult had been required of all as the condition for the toleration of the alien religions. Only the Jews enjoyed exemption, after the failure of Caligula to compel them like all others to obey the common law, though under Trajan their hitherto active missionary propaganda was restricted.

The tolerance commonly ascribed to the Romans rested on two facts: one was the freedom accorded to the foreign cults, even though absolutely contingent upon acceptance of emperor worship; the other was that emperor worship required only the external act of sacrifice and did not affect freedom of thought. He who performed the act could then think what he liked, and he might even mock the gods on his way to the temple. The deed counted, not the word. Judged by the standards of that time the Romans were intolerant rather than tolerant, and this was true not only during the persecution of the Christians—which might be regarded as exceptional—but in all times and places.

6

This is the crucial point in differentiating the essential in Roman religion from the peripheral. That from which no deviation was allowed and against which no rebellion was permitted—that was the core. Everything else was considered nonessential and might be left to the whim of individuals. He who was willing to yield or collaborate in essentials might be allowed to deviate on matters not expressly forbidden. This means, however, that freedom was granted only on the fringes of religion. The nonessential was the area of Roman tolerance.

Two examples abundantly illustrate Roman thought and practice. Both are well known, both significant, both characteristic for later Roman development. They reveal the conscious and unconscious principles determining Roman policy. The first is the letter of Pliny the younger, the proconsul of Bithynia in Asia Minor, to the emperor Trajan. The second consists of the edicts of the emperor Diocletian. At the peak and at the end of the old Roman empire one discovers the same impelling forces.

The famous letter of Pliny describes his dealings with the Christians:

> I asked them whether they were Christians. If they confessed, I posed the question a second and a third time with threat of penalty. Those who persisted I ordered to be executed, for I doubted not that whatever they professed, their persistence and inflexible obstinacy deserved to be punished.

7

. . . Those who denied that they were or ever had been Christians, and who after my example called upon the gods and supplicated your statue with wine and incense . . . and who in particular cursed Christ, all of which I hear those that are really Christians cannot be forced to do—these I considered should be released.[2]

This account shows with absolute clarity what was involved. The accused must sacrifice to the emperor and curse Christ—his person, not his teaching. What a Christian professed did not matter. Ideas, thoughts, and even words meant nothing. Roman intolerance was not directed against a teaching. Not belief but cultus was the ground of offense, and on this point the demand was stringent—he who refused was executed. The accused was confronted with the decision of life and death.

Trajan, the very pattern of the "good emperors," approved of the procedure. The Roman empire in the hands of its best representatives, *especially* in their

2. *Epistulae*, ed. C. F. W. Müller (Leipzig, 1903), pp. 291 ff., Epistle 10.96:  3. Interrogavi ipsos, an essent Christiani. Confitentes iterum ac tertio interrogavi, supplicium minatus; perseverantes duci iussi. Neque enim dubitabam, qualiscumque esset quod faterentur, pertinaciam certe et inflexibilem obstinationem debere puniri. 5. Qui negabant esse se Christianos aut fuisse, cum praesente me deos appellerent et imagini tuae, quam propter hoc iusserem cum simulacris numinum adferri, ture ac vino supplicarent, praeterea male dicerent Christo, quorum nihil posse cogi dicuntur qui sunt re vera Christiani, dimettendos esse putavi.

hands, never relinquished the religious foundations upon which it rested. The most circumspect ruler would never have thought to call them into question; to do so would have seemed to him utterly subversive. One who would not recognize the religious character of the state and refused to sacrifice to the emperor could be regarded only as a criminal and a rebel. There could be no talk of freedom of the faith for a minority whose very pretentions seemed to threaten the religious foundation of the state; and especially when times of crisis prompted reflection, no evidence of previous loyalty could shield from the sharpest measures a group that imperiled the cult of the state.

The most important witness is Diocletian, who reconstructed the empire after a long period of disorder. His edicts against the Christians are not extant, but he gave expression to these principles of the Roman faith in a succession of other edicts not directed expressly against the Christians but sufficient in scope to affect them also. These edicts thus serve to supply the reasons for the persecution of the Christians. In his edict on marriage Diocletian said, "What the Roman laws determined as pure and holy is honorable and must ever be observed with piety." [3] Only then can we "assume with confidence that the immortal gods will remain gracious to the Roman name." [4] Even

3. *Mosaicarum et Romanarum Legum Collectio* 6.4.1: Quoniam piis religiosisque mentibus nostris ea, quae Romanis legibus caste sancteque sunt constituta, venerabilia maxime videntur atque aeterna religione servanda.

4. *Fragmenta Vaticana*, ed. P. Krueger (1890), p. 157.

more clear is the Edict against the Manichees. "The old religion is not to be reproached by a new religion." "It is the greatest crime to renounce and impede that which was determined and established by the ancients and has had until now an unbroken course." [5] "Therefore we are determined to punish the infamous obstinacy [6] of evil men who oppose new and unheard-of sects to the worship of the gods, and according to their shameful caprice destroy that which the gods once and for all have committed unto us." [7]

Diocletian was fearful for the "modest and peaceable Roman people," whom he would protect from this alien poison. Therefore he inflicted the severest punishment. The leaders among the Manichees should be burned, together with their writings. The members

5. *Mos. et Rom. Leg. Coll.* 15.3.2: Maximi enim criminis est retractare quae semel ab antiquis statuta et definita suum statum et cursum tenent ac possident.

6. The inflexible obstinacy in the Christians of which Pliny had complained (above, p. 7) recurs here in the Manichees, and now the command that requires compliance is justified as that of the gods and the forebears. Obedience to the state is at once a moral and a religious duty.

7. The Christian reply to the deification of the past appears to be a repudiation of filial piety, because even the ancestors were in error. Lactantius pours scorn on the exaggerated regard for the judgments of the ancient: Ad maiorum iudicia confugiant, quod illi sapientes fuerint, illi probaverint, illi scierint quid esset optimum, seque ipsos sensibus spoliant, ratione abdicant, dum alienis erroribus credunt (*Div. Inst.* 5.19.3, cited by J. Moreau, *Lactance: De la mort des persécuteurs*, Sources Chrétiennes, 39 (Paris, 1954), 389. In the same way the reformers rejected the appeal of the Church to its ancient origin. Within limits, the appeal to antiquity has its rights, but not if these limits are exceeded.

of the sect could hope only for a milder death. Their property was to be confiscated. "The pestilence of this wickedness should be routed out from our auspicious age." [8] Throughout the whole of the Middle Ages, these laws were retained. Among all the heretical sects none was treated so severely as the Manichees and their successors, the Cathari.

This harshness in the time of Diocletian rested on the resolve to maintain a religious interpretation of the empire. The idea of Rome received here, at the end of its history, its clearest expression. The continuance of the empire was seen to depend inextricably on unshaken adherence to that which once and for all had been given; any deviation was worthy of death. The Romans deified their own past unable to discover a new way.

For us it is important that Diocletian did not set forth his view of the essence of the Roman empire in his Edict against the Christians but did so rather in another context without reference to the recent encounter of the empire with the Church. His principles were not devised as war measures valid only in exceptional circumstances. But it goes without saying that sooner or later they were bound to be applied to the Christians, and it is no accident that the emperor began with the court and the army in his attempt to purge all non-Roman elements.[9] The persecution commenced in the army, or had there its prelude. All

8. *Fragm. Vatic.*, p. 187.
9. Cf. Doerries, *Konstantin der Grosse* (see below, Bib. Note), pp. 11 f.

officers and not a few soldiers were confronted with a choice of sacrifice or dismissal. The pillars of the empire had to be stabilized by being founded on the cultus that would ensure the favor of the gods.

The explanation which most readily suggests itself to our age—that the Christians were excluded because as soldiers they were unreliable—is not adequate to the situation. The point was rather to establish a secure bond between the world below and the world above. The unadulterated cult of the old gods had to be kept intact, at least at the center of the empire—at the court and in the army—if the wrath of heaven were not to plague the empire.

As noted, the edicts of the great persecution have not come down to us. We know only their sequence, not their assumptions. But these are precisely our concern, rather than the external course and the disruptive consequences. We restrict our inquiry to the presuppositions and to the question how far they reached and how firmly they were grounded. Here a point of prime significance is that Diocletian apparently resolved to launch the attack on the Christian Church only after lengthy deliberation. He was fully aware of the difficulties. But after all the hesitation his final resolve shows that he regarded the clash as unavoidable, if his life's work were not to remain incomplete and insecure. The persons involved—the emperor and his attendants—as well as the moment chosen for the attack all go to show that the breach was irreconcilable. He who was guilty of tolerating that which challenged the very essence of the empire could only be regarded as a traitor, because a religious state neither will nor can be tolerant of another faith.

Nor is it our assignment to describe the barbarities inspired by the intolerance of the great persecution. The *Acts of the Martyrs*, even after the later legendary material has been expunged, disclose the horrors.[1] Undoubtedly all the powers of darkness that are unleashed in such a time contributed: mass hysteria, hate, vindictiveness, envy, and cruelty. But not only were passions let loose and not only was it the mob which raged. When the sign was given by the highest human order of justice, the finest spirits in the empire gave approbation. The Neoplatonist philosopher Hierocles appears to have been demoted from a high civil post to one of lower rank for the very reason that he might conduct the trials of the Christians with implacable severity. His philosophic coolness, one assumes, would not have been overcome by any considerations of mere humanity. The inner necessity of what took place in a sequence dictated step by step by unbreakable logic is the most frightful as well as the most significant aspect of the persecution. We have the feeling as we watch that we are looking upon an ineluctable drama.

What impresses us is the inevitability of what happened. The initial attempt of the emperor to avoid bloodshed led step by step through an inner necessity to frightful bloodshed and the disruption of all the

1. Cf. *Ausgewaehlte Maertyrerakten*, ed. R. Knopf and G. Krueger, 3d ed. 1929.

orders of the empire, for the device which sought to save proved disruptive. The "realistic" intolerance of the religiously oriented empire turned out to be highly unrealistic and precipitated a debacle. It was this aspect of the dismal spectacle which impressed the next generation as of chief significance because it spelled the end of an era.

To grant or refuse tolerance is the province of the mighty.[2] Tolerance and toleration are affairs of the state and of its maintenance, and only the convictions of those in power determine what will be done. At the same time the convictions of the persecuted are not negligible, first because they may induce the persecutors to grant tolerance, secondly because the persecuted may themselves some day come into power, and should they become intolerant, they may be confounded by the very words of their forebears. Yet in the moment of persecution the wielders of power make the decisions. Their principles are determinative; and that is why the tolerance which in the end was granted despite the Roman faith is the more remarkable. The breach with the past whether perceived or

2. One can properly speak of release, indulgence, and tolerance only if some other course is possible. Tolerance is exercised by the mighty, upon whom depends the freedom of him who is tolerated. To be sure, in modern times there is a distinction between tolerance and toleration, the former referring to a latitudinarian attitude, the latter to an act of forbearance. He who asks for toleration may seek to persuade the one in a position to exercise it, but that one alone can make the decision. That is why in the narrower sense tolerance belongs to the state.

not, is the more striking because the very emperor who came out for toleration was one of the most implacable representatives of Roman intolerance, and advocated this intolerance even when he conceded toleration.

Galerius, the heir and successor of Diocletian, had been the chief instigator of the persecution. Yet it was he who on his deathbed in April 311 rescinded the persecution which had been defeated by the stead-fastness of the martyrs. His edict opened the prisons and the mines and allowed the captives to go free.[3] The emperor began with an account of the recent events, recognizing that the intolerance had produced an in-tolerable situation. To be sure, to save face he refrained from reference to the disruption of the empire which necessitated the recall of the edicts of persecution. The consideration adduced was that many subjects had given up all religious observance. They would not worship the heathen gods and were not permitted to worship their own. That was intolerable. Therefore the imperial clemency permitted the Christians to re-sume their own worship. The reservation that it must

3. Text in Lactantius, *De mortibus persecutorum*, ed. Moreau (n. 7, above), c. 34. For the commentary, besides the work of Moreau one may still use with profit the article of John R. Knipfing, "The Edict of Galerius (A.D. 311) Recon-sidered," *Revue Belge de Philologie et d'Histoire*, *1* (1922), 693–705—except that Knipfing's opinion is not tenable that Galerius was reproaching the Christians with failure to recog-nize the principle of the Roman law according to which all foreign cults had a national character. His complaint, that the Christians "per diversa varios populos congregarent," refers to their wide expansion, not to their international character.

be in accord with the *disciplina* of the state was, however, capable of a wider application and might give rise to new measures of coercion. For the moment a second proviso was more important—that the Christians should intercede with their God for the emperor and the empire. This demand was rendered possible by the comprehensiveness of paganism; for just as other oriental deities had been adopted into the Roman Pantheon, so one might hope to enlist for the state the favor of this new god through the worship of his devotees. If at the same time one thought to preserve the ancient foundations of the state, then, to be sure, one was not alert to the tension that had been introduced. It was simply not possible to relinquish Diocletian's policy only as to the Christians and to retain the rest of his program, though the attempt was made: Galerius was so far from receding fundamentally from Diocletian that even now he justified the right of persecution.

In his Edict of Toleration he declared:

> Among the measures we have constantly undertaken for the public good we desired a general reform in accord with the ancient laws and public discipline of the Romans, and we sought even to recall to sanity the Christians who had seceded from the religion of their ancestors, for these Christians have for some reason been seized by such obstinacy and stupidity that not only did they not follow the usage of the ancients, which

16

perhaps their own parents instituted, but according to their own whim and caprice they made and observed laws for themselves and in divers places assembled all manner of men.[4]

The revocation of persecution was therefore not, as the Church Fathers claimed, an act of penance.[5] The emperor admitted a mistake, not a fault. The new religion had achieved recognition by its steadfast nonviolent resistance, but the interpretation of the new religion and the response to it were based on the old assumptions. These assumptions, however, did not meet the new situation and were therefore betrayed into inner contradiction.

The revocation of Galerius was the first step in the process of transition—significant, revealing, but insufficient. The next step was taken by Constantine. The victor at the Milvian Bridge, together with his brother-in-law, Licinius, issued a new edict of toleration.[6] The so-called Edict of Milan [7] goes back to a conference in which both emperors laid the ground for joint action, particularly in the matter of religion:

4. Lactantius, *De mortibus persecutorum* 34, ed. Moreau, pp. 116–17.

5. Ibid. 33.11: tandem malis domitus deum coactus est confiteri. Eusebius, *Historia ecclesiastica* 8.16.3.

6. "Toleration" meant for Constantine either *indulgentia* or, as in the Edict of Milan, *libera potestas* or *facultas* to follow the religion of one's choice.

7. The best edition of the Latin text with the parallels from the Greek version of Eusebius is to be found in Moreau

When I, Constantine Augustus, and I, Licinius Augustus, came by divine favor together at Milan and took under advisement that which pertains to the public weal and security, among other matters conducive to the general welfare we deemed a prime place should be given to the worship of divinity, and that we should grant to the Christians and to all men freedom to follow the religion of each man's choice, that whatever divinity there be in heaven be gracious and propitious to us and to all beneath our sway. Therefore we believe we should enter upon this course which is dictated by sound and entirely just reason that no one whatsoever should be denied the liberty of following the way of the Christians or any religion with which he is in most accord, that the highest divinity whose veneration we observe with free minds may accord to all his accustomed favor and benevolence.

Then the emperors removed the restrictions hitherto imposed upon the Christians. These measures "utterly malign and foreign to our clemency may be annulled, and now any whatever who desire to observe the cult of the Christians may do so freely and without disturbance or molestation. . . . We have granted to these same Christians the free and absolute exercise of their cult. Likewise we have accorded open and free observance to other cults in accord with the tranquillity

(n. 7, above), with a French translation and an extensive commentary, c. 48, pp. 131-35.

of our times." The emperors decreed the restitution of Christian places of worship and of other corporate property. "By this means the divine favor we have experienced in such great events will continue to bless the commonwealth with success for all time."

We cannot here go into the difficult problems of the two versions in which the law has come down to us. They were published by Licinius immediately after his victory over Maximinus Daza, his rival in the East, and refer—not without redundance and ineptitude—to what had been determined upon at Milan, of which an account is given.[8]

8. After the Battle of the Milvian Bridge the senate recognized the victor as the first Augustus, though in point of rank he was the youngest of the three. So incontestable was Constantine's superiority that the two others, for good or ill, had to accommodate themselves to this shift in rank. Licinius did so too. The edict he issued after his campaign against Maximinus Daza placed the name of Constantine first, and if the text did not expressly state that the essentials of his program had been worked out in oral consultation with Constantine, now his brother-in-law, this at any rate was implied. Even without documentary confirmation we may confidently assume that the most important question there to be settled was the future religious policy. Likewise it goes without saying that here if anywhere the judgment of the more powerful of the two was determinative. Though no record of the understandings there reached has survived, we should count it surprising if none were made. Both of the partners, the greater and the less, had an interest in safeguarding their actions and pronouncements from ambiguity. Constantine in particular had reason to clarify the directions governing the policy of his older rival, who cannot have submitted too happily to the conquering will of the ascending emperor in the West. There should be no re-

When we come to interpretation, we have the choice of three modes. The first is simply to recover what was actually decreed. That was the task of the provincial governors who were called upon to execute the order in terms solely of its legal content. The second mode is to regard the edict from the point of view of the biography of Constantine and inquire what the document means for his development. In this case an effort must be made, with the aid of other contemporary documents, to determine just how much Constan-

---

lapse into the abandoned system whose perversity had become sufficiently evident. All of this may be inferred from the situation and from the opening words of the edict, namely that Constantine held the rank of emperor number one, that the negotiations took place in Milan, and that the religious question was uppermost.

These points are evident also from the content. Although one may assume that some concessions were made to Licinius, the convinced sun worshiper, one can scarcely suppose that it was *he* who had experienced the favor of heaven "in matters so great" or that it was *he* who in thankfulness for victory had granted freedom to the Christians. A stronger spirit and a mightier hand was needed to conceive and express the thoughts which the document contains. The retarding hand of Licinius is apparent in the compromises of the whole. Nothing is said of the privileges accorded the Christian clergy, the imperial donations to the churches, or the restitution of private property. And the expression *quidquid divinitatis*, "whatever there be of divinity," is more open to a polytheistic than to a monotheistic interpretation. What Licinius regarded as a maximum was for Constantine a minimum. But in the emphasis placed upon a voluntary adherence to the worship of the godhead, later fully expressed as Constantine's most fundamental persuasion, another faith is manifest than the old Roman or the sun cult of Licinius.

tine had to do with it; then the document can be regarded as a compromise between the two divergent
views and can be split into its components. But we
must take a third mode. We must treat the epoch-
making edict as a whole and see what it can tell us of
its origin, aim, and presuppositions.

To begin with the most obvious, the Edict of Milan
restored the property of the Church, the places of religious assembly, and the cemeteries; and all restrictions
which had hitherto impeded the faith were removed.
These provisions were derived from the principle that
each should be given the freedom to choose his own
religion, whether Christianity or some other. The basis
for the freedom was that only so would the deity be
favorable and gracious. To assure for the state the
indispensable favor of heaven was the avowed intent
of the new religious policy.

The Edict of Milan, by seeking to maintain the cultic
security of the state, remained within the ancient and
traditional frame of religious thought. The favor of
heaven with which the mightiest emperor could not
dispense and on which indeed his power rested must
be won and kept through correct worship. On this
point the Edict of Milan is akin to that of Galerius,
though in other respects the difference is great.
Whereas Galerius conceded to the Christians only
what he could no longer withhold, the Edict of Milan
accorded them positive favor. In the former decree the
emperor looked only for supplementary help from the
new cult, but in the latter the gift of freedom to the

Christians was deemed the primary reason for the continuance of divine grace to the empire. They were no longer on the fringe but under the full light. There can be no question that the great event in which the divine favor had lately been manifest was the conquest of Rome—all contemporary historians were agreed as to that. One may therefore ask whether it was not the sign of the cross under which the victory was attained which determined the Edict of Milan. One may also ask whether the voluntary dedication of the emperor to the worship of the godhead does not go back to Constantine's own experience, which now was to be made available to all.[9] These questions that confront

9. The significant phrase "whose religion we observe with free minds" is lacking in Eusebius. Was it expunged from the second edition on the ground that it was only the thought of Constantine? But on the other hand only Eusebius has the sharp word against the edicts now rescinded of the former emperors: ἅτινα πάνυ σκαιὰ καὶ τῆς ἡμετέρας πραότητος ἀλλότρια εἶναι ἐδόκει, ταῦτα ὑφαιρεθῇ. Moreau has taken over these words from the Latin translation of Valesius and has incorporated them into his valuable edition of Lactantius. As a matter of fact the Latin text does have a lacuna to be supplied from Eusebius, but Moreau's homoioteleuton *continebantur . . . videbantur* is not satisfactory, because the first part is derived from a new translation and because the end needs to be filled out. If the word of condemnation is lacking in the text of Lactantius, may it not be that Licinius or his official hesitated to leave in the version issued at Nikomedia such a blunt stigmatizing of the edict of Diocletian as σκαιός, sinister? Constantine certainly showed no reserve with regard to the sharpest rejection of the policy of his predecessors and especially Diocletian.

Moreau's contention that we have here to do with Maxus cannot be answered simply on the basis of the document itself, but the document assists our understanding, for an important difference comes to light if it be compared with the edict of Galerius, which was extracted by an emergency; whereas Milan, the crisis having passed, rested not on compulsion but on conviction.

The edict is the more remarkable because it would have been natural for a ruler after his conversion to Christianity to shift all the previous relations. But whatever may lie between the lines of the edict, they themselves give no preference to either of the two religions. One may be momentarily startled to find that the old cultus observed for centuries in the Roman empire should be referred to casually as "the religion of each man's choice." There is, however, no shadow cast on the old religion. In fact, instead of the term "godhead," used also by Christian theologians, we find a strictly pagan expression, "whatever divinity there be in Heaven." This phrase may well have been inserted by Licinius, who was a devotee of the sun god. But throughout the edict the two cults are accorded the

imian's Sabinus-Rescript has no warrant in the text. Rather, he correctly refers to the emperors the ἡμῶν of the earlier γράμματα, which should not be restricted, as Moreau restricts it, to Licinius.

The version of Eusebius, especially the preamble, has much not to be found in the version composed by Lactantius at Nikomedia. The two versions supplement each other, and as H. Nesselhauf has shown, in "Das Toleranzgesetz des Licinius," *Historisches Jahrbuch*, 79 (1955), they disclose as their common source the protocol at Milan.

same right. Both the old and the new are to ensure the continuance of divine grace and enjoy unimpeded access to the godhead. The empire rests upon both ways of worshiping God. It is an ellipse with two foci. The edict thus fulfills the need of both the inner and the outer situation. That is why it merits the attention given to it in history.

A third word was spoken in this period of transition. It was not comparable to the other two, but it discloses another possibility and therefore serves to clarify the edicts of Milan and Galerius. It was contained in the edicts of Maximinus Daza, a nephew of Galerius and the ruler of the southeastern portion of the empire. Up to this point his name had been blackened by particularly savage persecutions, from which he desisted only when restrained by pressures from his superiors, first the Edict of Toleration of Galerius and then the policy of Constantine and Licinius. The edicts issued under the name of Maximinus have only a specious independence.[10] When acting for himself, he adhered to the principle that the welfare of the state depends upon the favor of the gods, whose worship therefore remains a necessity. And even when, under pressure, he disclaimed the forcible measures he had instigated, he nevertheless avowed very clearly that his intent had been to win back the apostates to the worship of the gods. The blame for the persecution was indeed shifted to the decree of Diocletian, which he

10. For the edicts of Maximinus Daza see Doerries, *Das Selbstzeugnis Kaiser Konstantins* (see Bib. Note, below), pp. 232 ff.

had been obliged to obey, or to despotic judges, or to the interference of subordinates. Maximinus even justified himself on the ground that there were some cities which desired no Christians within their walls. How could he refuse this their wish? His own share in soliciting the wish was discreetly passed over. How little reliance could be placed upon his edicts of toleration appears from a bronze inscription preserved at Tyre. Here, as previously, the city was praised for the desire to be free of Christians. This pious disposition of the city and of the emperor was to be maintained for all time. From this inscription one can see that the tolerance conceded under pressure would be abrogated at the first convenient occasion. It was a case of tactical retreat before a constellation of power, not a case of personal decision. Tolerance through lack of principles is also a possibility in a period of transition.

What then happened after the Battle of Chrysopolis which made Constantine sole ruler of the empire? His war against Licinius was a holy war. The more both sides in the preparation of the conflict brought religious issues to the fore and sought each to enlist the aid of the army of heaven, the more the defeat of the pagan emperor must have appeared to be proof of the impotence of his gods. The battle won beneath the Christian ensign made Constantine sole emperor of the Roman world. Should he not, then, deprive the heathen of every right? Instead, there followed something totally unexpected. The conclusion the emperor drew from his victory was a renewal of tolerance.

"Peace and quiet," he announced, "should be enjoyed by those who err as much as by believers. For this would bring them to the true faith. No one should molest another. Each should live according to his own persuasion." Constantine then proclaimed his principles in the form of a prayer: "Those who rightly believe should be assured that they alone live pure and holy lives whom Thou callest to fulfill Thy commandments. But those who withdraw themselves may keep the temple of error. We have the house lighted by Thy truth." This truth, he felt, was evident to all of right mind: "He who will not let himself be healed has only himself to blame, for the means of healing are manifest." But although the erring are without excuse, they are not to be constrained. "No one," the emperor continued, "should harm another on account of his own persuasion. Whenever possible, what one has seen and known should be used for the benefit of the neighbor, but if that cannot be, let him go in peace." And then comes the climactic sentence: "The battle for deathlessness requires willing recruits. Coercion is of no avail."

These passages appear in an encyclical the victorious emperor addressed to the new provinces.[1] It was his own faith that Constantine here confessed. But he was convinced that he was voicing only that which had been valid from the very beginning of the world as to

1. *Vita Constantini* 2.48–60, and, esp., 2.56 ff., ed. Ivar A. Heikel; "Eusebius Werke," I, *Die griechischen christlichen Schriftsteller der ersten drei Jahrhunderte* (Leipzig, 1902), p. 61, line 20, to p. 65, line 25. Cf. *Selbstzeugnis*, pp. 51 ff.

the true worship of God. To be sure, it had been obscured and had had to be brought again to life through the Son of God. Yet nature and the law of nature witnessed as much to its truth as did the events of this generation. "Therefore O Lord I have brought Thee my soul in love and fear. I sincerely love Thy name and fear Thy power which Thou hast manifested in diverse ways and by which Thou hast confirmed my faith." [2] Such faith laid upon him the duty of its realization. Constantine envisaged an empire at peace and religiously united. To achieve it, he needed the help of the Christians. He would himself restore the holy house of God damaged during the persecution.

One would suppose that this resolve would have led inevitably to the establishment of the Church as the only religion in the empire and to the suppression of temple worship. But instead of such a decree there came an edict of toleration. Its form is remarkable because it is couched as a prayer. Only to God is an explanation given. And this recognition of answerability to Him alone lifts the matter out of the realm of discussion.

The personal conviction of the emperor voices an unequivocal judgment of disapproval on the ancient cultus. Without reservation he says that there is no healing there and the ancient shrines are but "the temples of error." The heathen are the erring, and since they have withdrawn from the commands of God they are also subject to moral condemnation. Not as in the

2. *Vita Constantini* 2.55; ed. Heikel, p. 63, line 32.

Edict of Milan, the emperor now clearly declares himself to be a Christian, for "*we* have the house lighted by Thy truth." The heathen cult is thus sharply rejected. If formerly the door to deity was open for the heathen, now it is closed. Not a kernel of truth remains.

But however clearly truth and falsehood divide, the freedom of the erring is not to be restricted. They enjoy a full share in the benefits of peace which now, at the end of the civil war, accrue to all citizens of the empire. If they have lost their heavenly right, the earthly remains intact. Even their temples are not to be taken away from them. They may frequent them without molestation. The right of worship is freely assured.

The rejection on the one hand and the freedom on the other are combined in a tolerance of persuasion bidding all who err to enter the Church. Constantine did not think of this coexistence of two different religions as something to last indefinitely. The ideal of the unity of all men in the worship of the one God applied also to those who for the present abstained. Although the way could be trodden only voluntarily, the emperor hoped that those who till then had held aloof would soon join. To this end participation in the blessings of the new era might be of help. The lesson of history, so evident to him, might speak also to others. This was itself one of the means of healing whose power the emperor declared to be "manifest."

It was at this point that Constantine turned to the Christians. From those whose cause had been vindicated he expected something. As he exhorted them to prove their faith by their life, so he laid upon them a task that reached beyond their circle: "What one has seen and known should be used for the benefit of the neighbor." But while he attributed missionary power to the Christian witness, he sought at the same time to protect the heathen from any assault. There were limits. The roles were not to be reversed, and the Christians were not to do what had been done to them. "No one should use that of which he had come to be persuaded to another's hurt." The proposition that "each should live according to his own persuasion" excludes any sort of injury, let alone force to be applied to nonbelievers. If one could not persuade another, let him go his way. This course was dictated not only by the requirements of the public peace but also by the very nature of faith itself.

The words addressed to the Christians and to the heathen correspond to each other. Neither were irreconcilable promises made to each side, nor were the questions as to coexistence evaded. The freedom promised the heathen for the exercise of their religion corresponded to the heightened duty of tolerance laid upon the Christians. The imperial judgment that the heathen were in error corresponded to the injunction to the Christians to testify to their faith. Because Constantine ascribed compelling power to peaceful means, there could be no permanent lines drawn between Christians and heathen.

"The battle for deathlessness requires willing recruits. Coercion is of no avail." [3] This is his own formulation of the Christian teaching that faith cannot be compelled. The statement, uttered by Tertullian on behalf of the persecuted to the government that denied them tolerance, stressed the point that force can secure only outward compliance, not inner persuasion. Constantine's statement belongs in another context. He was asserting the ground for his counsel to let the unpersuaded neighbor go in peace. He would forestall any infraction of the conquered faith by the conquering, just as he enjoined moderation upon the state. His word was directed to those who should exercise tolerance rather than to those who demanded it.

It is "the battle for deathlessness" that demands freedom—the more remarkable because Constantine's religion was so this-worldly. Yet at the point where faith enters upon a kingdom beyond the sword of the state, the very notion of coercing faith becomes unthinkable. Everyone must consent here to freedom. We do not need to inquire as to the quality of faith by which

3. The hope of immortality is elsewhere not alien to the thought of Constantine. In his communication of the results of Nicaea to the congregations he based this hope upon the celebration of Easter: τὴν ἑορτὴν ταύτην, παρ' ἧς τὴν τῆς ἀθανασίας εἰλήφαμεν ἐλπίδα (ibid. 3.18.1; ed. Heikel, p. 85, line 6). He reminded the Arian bishop Theodotos of Laodicea, Nov./Dec. 325—Athanasius 3.28, ed. Hans-Georg Opitz, "Athanasius Werke," *Urkunden zur Geschichte des Arianischen Streites, 3,* No. 1 (Berlin and Leipzig, 1934)—that eternal life is the reward of victory. The martyrs strove for "heavenly hope": οἱ τὴν οὐράνιον ὀρθῶς μεταδιώξαντες ἐλπίδα (*Vita Constantini,* 2.29.2; ed. Heikel, p. 53, line 22).

Constantine was impelled or why he spoke of the "battle for deathlessness." Enough that this expression suited him and his position. This was the firm basis of his toleration of the heathen. Such a policy, following directly on the decisive defeat of the heathen emperor, was not in accord neither with the prevailing trend nor the religious and political expectations of the time. This was Constantine's own word and was contrary even to the wishes of the Christians. They, too, had read the lessons of history and interpreted them in no other way than did their emperor. God Himself, through his servant the emperor, had overthrown the powers of darkness and saved the world from corruption. Could one fail to see the obvious deduction to be drawn from this event? Would not one be inviting a repetition of the disaster if one should allow the temples of the ancient gods to remain open? Constantine took up this objection in the conclusion to his address. "I hear," he said, "some are saying that the power of darkness and the worship in the temples have been broken." [4] He, too, wished that this worship might cease and that the heathen would acknowledge the truth. No more, as in the Edict of Milan, did he expect anything from the old cultus for the benefit of the empire. Like the Christians he saw in it, rather, a menace. His counsel must therefore be to abstain from it. But the wish to close the temples he would not endorse. "I would recommend it," said he, "were not the corrupted and refractory error prejudicial to universal

4. *Vita Constantini* 2.60.

salvation so deeply ingrained in some souls." [5] In this statement, with which he repulsed the petition addressed to him, he turned from the cultus to the men who observed it. The faith of all men sets the boundary to force. The voluntariness of faith, which the Edict of Milan had recognized in favor of the Christians, must now be brought by the emperor to their own attention. "The battle for deathlessness requires willing recruits. Coercion is of no avail."

Constantine acted in accord with these words. Worship in the temples continued and the heathen were not pushed aside. Now as before he admitted them to the highest offices. Officials no longer had to sacrifice and the imperial cult was of course discontinued, but it was not replaced by obligatory Christian rites which the heathen could not render. From the Christian viewpoint public officials had no priestly function. Precisely this separation of the priestly and the political enabled the heathen to retain a political role. What a profound change this separation was to exercise, the following centuries were to show. At their close the secularized state emerged.

The conclusion of the emperor's message pointed to the fact that many were still enmeshed in heathenism —the majority of the population in fact. Political sagacity alone therefore precluded interference with the religious practices of the heathen subject; but the reason the emperor adduced in his appeal to God was different. "Faith itself admits of no constraint." This

5. Ibid.

principle permitted Constantine to do what the situation required: just as the Christian separation of function enabled the heathen to remain in office, so also the command of faith gave the emperor freedom to retain them.

Such a weighty word as the statement "the battle for deathlessness requires willing recruits" does not say very much unless it grows out of the experience of him by whom it is spoken. Constantine's proclamation of tolerance rested on his own history. Freedom to go his own way was exactly what he had exercised.

His course had begun with silent disapproval of the Christian persecutions on which Diocletian resolved at the end of his reign. The young prince Constantine, reared as a hostage at the court of the old emperor, whose policy he was in many respects later to continue and fulfill, at this point rejected the coercive religious program of his teacher, since it robbed the empire of useful members and loosed savagery against worthy men. Here one sees the sure and independent judgment of the incipient statesman, as well as his moral indignation against injustice. Still, at that time he was not moved by any approach to the faith of the persecuted. As a soldier he admired the steadfastness of the martyrs and sensed in them a sustaining power. The consequences of the disastrous policy of the empire were not slow in following. To Constantine as to others the ill fortune and decline of the persecutors appeared as a divine judgment.

The return of Constantine to his father in Britain and succession to him in the government carried with it exclusion of Christian persecution from his portion of the empire. The first years of his administration provided an opportunity to act in accord with his early aversion to constraint. On his part this was a period of seeking, during which he still adhered to the cult of the sun god. Constantine's final decision included an insight into the moral order of the universe, which he interpreted as a conversion and a daring resolve to throw himself into the battle for Rome under the Christian ensign. This purely personal decision had no prototype. Here was an act of independence over against the past which clave the unity of the Roman empire and the Roman religion. No less independent was the manner in which he grasped the Christian faith. He did not attach himself to a group of people in whose institutional structure and dynamism his clairvoyant eye perceived a future political asset. Rather, he committed himself to the God worshiped by the Christians, and even while they held aloof from politics he expected help from their God for political ends. The new way upon which he had entered and which took its course through the victory at Rome and the sole rulership of the emperor seemed to him to have begun and ended under divine leadership. Just as he had gone over an untrodden course and perceived the powerlessness of external compulsion, so also he would give to his subjects the freedom of personal decision.

34

An incisive law does not as such invest an hour of history with supreme historical rank, nor does an event which is not understood, however far-reaching its consequences. But when the word and the deed come together and the great event is grasped in a great manner, then one can speak of stature in history.

Constantine, after the victory at Chrysopolis, which brought unity to the empire, turned to the eastern provinces in order to explain to them the meaning of this hour. A review of recent history served as an aid to comprehension. He could point out that the persecution of Diocletian—contrary as it was to law and to God—had brought disaster to the state. And the task of restoration God Himself had given to the emperor. With such authority and under the Christian ensign, Constantine had then not only defeated the disturbers of the peace but had cast down the demonic power sustaining them, the great dragon of the abyss. The reference here is obviously to the great events which had been the experience of all. His subjects should not be blind to that which lay evident to all. The demand of the hour, whose herald he was, had to be fulfilled with all the powers of soul and mind. The personal confession of the emperor should be appropriated by his subjects and made their own because his history was their history also. The hour called for more than conservation of the past. They also had to look to the future, into which the emperor was leading them, but where they could follow only through their own decision.

This view of history, the confession, and the appeal all prove the seriousness of his proclamation of freedom. They would have had no point if mere command and blind obedience could have sufficed. The intelligent cooperation necessary for the achievement of the emperor's goal required freedom of faith.

Here it is that the history of the emperor is conjoined with universal history. Here it is that the widest dimension was achieved from the world below to the world above. Political history was understood as religious history. There is here an understanding of history derived from faith and issuing in faith. This in itself calls for freedom. To assess the significance of Constantine's stand, we must scan a vast expanse from a height sufficient to enable us to take in its totality. Let us bring before ourselves what it entailed. The peculiar quality lay not in the new form contributed to the Roman empire, for at this point Diocletian had already made the beginning which Constantine merely brought to completion. Rather, the newness lay in that something believed impossible had come to pass; that the emperor had become a Christian; that the Church and the empire had found each other; that in this moment the history of their union through more than sixteen centuries had its beginning—this is why the Constantinian era was epoch-making. With a single stroke, that which hitherto had exercised rulership had been dethroned. That which had been built for eternity collapsed overnight. That which formerly had been deemed holy was branded as unholy, and the despised came to be honored. There was no height this change did not scale and no depth it did not plumb. And in this moment, when the victory of Constantine over Licinius demolished the last rampart of antiquity and a new period definitely began, precisely at this moment there was a check. Tolerance seemed to impede the new and rescue the old from eradication. But the preservation of the old was not due to the old, as if the conquered could lay down the law to the conqueror, but rather sprang from the nature of the new and is to be understood only on this basis. This tolerance legislated for the actual situation, but it was not a political word, as if the statesman simply bowed to necessity. Nor was it derived from principles lying readily at hand. It was precisely to the Christians that the emperor had to address his explanation. He had responded to the demand of faith, which left him free to deal with the situation as the case required. His proclamation was at once his own word and yet not his own contrivance. It fashioned the hour and gave to it its stature in history. It lifted the hour above the flow of events, gave to the old its due, and could claim to be acknowledged as fruition by the new.

The most indisputable proof of the genuineness of Constantine's tolerance is the treatment of worship in the army. This was still considered to be as important for the security of the state as in the days of the heathen emperors. Diocletian and Galerius removed the Christians from the army because their very presence imperiled the sacrifices and deprived them of their efficacy. For the same reason later Theodosius II allowed only Christians to serve in the army, because the heathen by their presence would alienate heavenly assistance.

The regulation of worship in the army lay with the emperor. Now was the time to see whether Constantine would hold true to his principle, when it was a question of keeping or of losing power, since everything depended on assuring the help of Him who determines the outcome of battles. A solution was not easy to find, because the heathen cult no longer had any access to heaven; yet no one should be forced to take part in Christian worship.

The emperor sought a middle course. On Sundays, when the Christian soldiers were occupied with their services, the pagans were assembled on an open field and were summoned to engage in a common prayer. Constantine himself composed the text. "We know that Thou alone art God, we acknowledge Thee as King, we lift our hands to Thee as our helper. Thine outstretched arm hath given us the victory. Through Thee we were stronger than our enemy. We thank Thee for Thy help vouchsafed in time past and beseech it for the future. Grant for our sakes unto our emperor Constantine and his beloved sons length of days, health and victory." [6]

Only a monotheistic prayer—Constantine was sure

6. *Vita Constantini* 4.20; ed. Heikel, p. 125, line 7.

of that—would be well received; and since the heathen recognized the supreme deity, the emperor assumed that non-Christians would not take umbrage if he placed in pagan mouths a prayer to the Emperor in Heaven. They should pray to Him as their helper in battle and ask of Him victory, as Constantine himself had done in a critical hour with such evident success. Through such a prayer they would at the same time reinforce the power of the earthly emperor and assure the continuance of his house.

This was an astonishing solution, which must be evaluated in the light of the views of the period. It shows that the emperor had in no sense relinquished his judgment as to the uselessness of the heathen cultus, and at the same time that he was not false to his conviction that true faith cannot be forced. He allowed the Christians to attend their own worship and did not require that they take part in a neutral and syncretistic celebration, but neither did he compel the heathen to enter the church. They must take part in the religious worship serviceable to the state but need not compromise their own conscience.

Judged in terms of the period and its assumptions, Constantine's prayer for the army is a proof of the genuineness of his tolerance.

A backward look now at the Edict of Milan will enable us to perceive the special quality of Constantine's Edict of Toleration. That which Milan adumbrated here becomes clear—namely the emperor's personal Christian confession, on the basis of which he addresses all and summons all to follow his way. This determines his judgment that the Christians are right and the heathen are in error. The heathen temples are temples of falsehood. The powers of darkness reign therein. In this document he leaves the heathen no access to heaven, as he had done at Milan. For whereas then he assumed that the practice of their cultus could be a benefit to the empire, now he thinks that it is rather a peril. But alongside the sharp rejection stands an unrestricted freedom: the heathen are not forbidden to frequent the temples.

At the same time—and this was a point that Milan did not envisage—Christian and heathen are brought into relation with each other. Christians are enjoined to address themselves to the heathen in order to benefit them by their knowledge and experience. But if the heathen reject the message, they are to be permitted to go their own way—just as the emperor himself addresses them in terms of his own experience and insight and when they close their ears exercises no constraint. The duty to speak and the command to be silent and leave alone affects alike the emperor and the Christians whom he addresses. They have a part in his tolerance and he in their witness. He is not a third party above the two religions. He belongs to the one over against the other, with responsibility both as an emperor and as a Christian.

This was a provisional regulation looking to a not far distant future in which it would be superfluous. But this very provisional character contained the warrant of continuance, because the hope by which it was limited proved deceptive. In contrast with the Edict of Milan, the transitional quality of the later edict becomes evident. Cast in a form without specific limitation and so apparently valid forever, it became obsolete with the passing of the epoch in terms of which it was conceived and to which it was addressed. Constantine's law for the pagan, however, because not bound to the moment to which it was directed, acquired its place in history.

But in changing the second focal point of Milan into an exclusive center, did not the edict of 324 really return to that of Galerius, except that now the Christian Church took the place of the pagan temple? The tolerance which Galerius had extended to the Christians was now bestowed upon the pagans. But both thought in terms of a circle and not—like Milan —an ellipse. Of course, Galerius' concession had been made under the pressure of the state's emergency and expected in return that Christian intercession would procure additional heavenly help for the Empire. By contrast, Constantine's toleration took place at the height of his power and sought no gain from the temple's adherents. The Edict of Milan like that of Galerius put its hope in both religions, but it was distinguished from that of Galerius by the sure confidence placed in Christian worship. This represented an advance over Galerius in the history of toleration. On the other hand, the untroubled continuance of both cults from now on depended upon the continuance of imperial confidence in the rights of both. Should this confidence be shaken, tolerance would be endangered. This state of affairs Licinius, one of the two signatories, soon made clear: he began to oppress the Christians. Constantine, too, lost confidence in the rights of one of the religions recognized by Milan. But while he returned to the conviction that it is only one cult which bears up the empire, he remained tolerant and even deepened his own understanding of toleration. It was this new understanding that guaranteed to those who were tolerated a measure of safety which even Milan could not provide for them. So the idea of toleration advanced to a new stage: appearing to return to Galerius, it nevertheless adopted the purpose of Milan and so united both within itself—and uniting, transcended them both.

Toward the end of his life Constantine was again confronted with the question of tolerance. This time it was not the Roman empire but the Persian Kingdom that was involved. Constantine addressed himself to Schapur II on behalf of the Christians who were being persecuted in his realm. In this document [7] he

7. Doubts as to the authenticity of the letter, "the Constantinian one above all" (Heinz Kraft, "Kaiser Konstantins religiöse Entwicklung," *Beiträge zur historischen Theologie*, *20*, Tübingen, 1955, p. 262), have recently grown weaker. It is not hard to dispose of the objection that a Roman emperor would not thus deliver his predecessor over to the national enemy and expressly mention the ignominious capture of the Emperor Valerian, since in the case of a persecutor over-

gave up all thought of a national religion. The view that each people and kingdom was protected by its own gods and could tolerate no foreign cult, a concept very common in the ancient world, finds no place here. The connection remains, to be sure, between the cultus and the favor of heaven. The good fortune and power of the state depends on more than the might of the army and the wisdom of the ruler. The right worship of God is indispensable for the well-being of the commonwealth. But the sharp critique directed against the old Roman cult does not spare the Persian. For now it has become apparent that the persecution of the people of God, the Christians, occasions the fall of the persecutors.

The fate of Constantine's predecessors should serve as a warning to the Persian monarch. No less should the conquering course of the Christian emperor serve as an example for Schapur's treatment of the Persian Christians. He would speedily learn what it means to win the Right Helper by granting to His adherents the royal favor—Constantine could abundantly testify to this out of the success and honor that had come to him. Counsels of political prudence pointed to the toleration of the Christians, whereas intolerance would avenge itself on the Persian empire.

The import of the ideas touched upon here goes far

---

thrown and ejected from the empire by God, there was no reason for triumph on the one side or revenge on the other, and this disgrace need therefore no longer stand in the way of a reconciliation between the Persians and the Romans.

beyond what the writer sees immediately before his eyes. If carried through, this principle demolishes the walls between the state and other nations and discloses to the other side the secret of one's power, thus removing in friendship the barriers by which hitherto the peoples have sought to protect themselves against one another. Constantine was not impelled by skepticism or relativism to champion religious liberty beyond the confines of his own territory. He did not concede the freedom of any belief whatsoever, as if it were not the affair of the state to meddle with personal persuasion. Nor did he confine his warning to pointing out that persecution may occasion rifts detrimental to the state. He was concerned for the true religion and the benefit that would accrue to the Great King who granted tolerance to its adherents, not simply because he would thereby win the willing loyalty of a portion of his subjects but because he would enjoy an intangible but very real increase in power through the grace of the God in heaven whom they worshiped. Constantine showed also how faith affects the morale of believers, how rulers and ruled experience an inner change; but the decisive points are not that the rulers are more responsible and modest and the ruled more reliable and law-abiding; the crux is the favor or wrath of the Almighty, who protects his own and punishes their persecutors. Constantine, who was persuaded by his own history and that of his time of the reality of an avenging Deity and of the might of His arm, gave in this letter a proof

44

of his faith when he disclosed the secret of his strength to the only foreign ruler he had any reason to fear. He behaved—to use a modern analogy—as if he were communicating to a rival the secret of the atom bomb.[8]

As long as he lived, Constantine adhered to the principles he had grasped and proclaimed, though to be sure his religious policy raises for us a number of questions and exhibits instances that make one wonder whether after all he was true to his principles. One such, the closing of a few temples of Venus, however, was prompted by the moral looseness of the cult and should be regarded as police action in the interests of public decency rather than a case of religious intolerance. And if Constantine permitted some golden idols to be melted and minted, this was done in the interest of the exchequer, precisely as under some pagan emperors. There is really only one case attested by his biographer and a pagan historian where Constantine violated the otherwise universal freedom: he destroyed a shrine of Aesculapius, for reasons which elude us.[9]

8. Leopold von Ranke, *Weltgeschichte*, *3*, Pt. I (Leipzig 1883), 531: "Die religiöse Wahrheit muss eine lebendige Repräsentatio haben, um den Staat in fortwährender Erinnerung an den Ursprung und das Ziel des irdischen Lebens, an das Recht seiner Nachbarn und die Verwandtschaft aller Nationen zu erhalten; er würde sonst in Gefahr sein, in Gewaltherrschaft auszuarten, in einseitigem Fremdenhass zu erstarren" (Ranke, introduction to his *Reformationsgeschichte* in his *Deutsche Geschichte im Zeitalter der Reformation*, ed. W. Andreas, 2 vols., Wiesbaden, 1957).

9. *Vita Constantini* 3.57. Libanius, *Oratio pro templis* 59.

Could it have been because the serpent there worshiped was for Constantine a too visible symbol of the demonic power he had overthrown? [1]

If on this occasion he leaned to the left, elsewhere his inclination was to the right. We cannot join Eusebius in praising the emperor because in a heathen city he gained adherence to the church of his construction by largess to the poor,[2] that the under- or overtones of silver might make Christian preaching resound more pleasantly in their ears; nor can we sanction the restoration of a small town in Asia Minor to municipal status basically because the majority of its inhabitants were Christians.[3]

These are details and of no great consequence. More influential and therefore more questionable was the behavior of the emperor in becoming himself a preacher. Even if he did not place his sword on the scales, his authority might induce many without reflection to follow his example. The door of the Church was now wide open and nothing impeded entrance. Many therefore streamed in the wake of the emperor, who otherwise held aloof.

But should one reproach Constantine because he

1. On Aesculapius in the form of a serpent consult Arnobius, *Adversus nationes* 7.44 ff., ed. Reifferscheid, *Corpus scriptorum ecclesiasticorum latinorum, 4* (Vienna, 1875), 278, lines 30 ff.

2. *Vita Constantini* 3.58. Eusebius does not hesitate to refer here not to the sermon but to the "conversion" and the imperial enticement.

3. Ibid. 4.38. Cf. *Selbstzeugnis*, pp. 212 ff.

gave expression to his faith? Should he not have advised everyone to enter with him into the "lighted House of Truth," so long as he foreswore coercion? He was himself convinced that he could offer no better counsel. He had himself experienced the power of God so mightily manifest in the events of his life. He was inviting his people to listen, as he had himself done, to the voice of fact. But this is just the point at which our misgivings are the most acute. We do not trust successes as if the voice of God were to be heard in the fanfare of victory; and if the persecuted achieve their rights, this is not the proof that they are right, even though we do speak of the judgments of God and have for ourselves experienced such. However thankful we may be for peace, we are not prepared to say that its enjoyment is itself the definitive vindication of the teaching which was for a time suppressed. But Constantine looked to the testimony of events as the surest confirmation of the faith, and pointed his subjects to this vindication as the irrefutable proof of the correctness of the Christian cause.[4]

4. The combination we have here of the testimony of the word with the voice of history and the power of the fellowship prompts one at first blush to ask whether such a reinforcement of the simple word is a rare exception in Church history or is the rule. The question is important and not easy to answer. But when one reflects that the elements with which the pure gold of the Gospel can fuse are numerous, one will see so many of such amalgamations in history as to eliminate occasion for surprise or shock. Are there, as in this instance, historical necessities; and if so where is the norm by which the obligatory, the possible, the permitted, and the forbidden

There were thus questions which Constantine left unanswered. The most serious among them have to do with his concept of religion rather than with his religious policy. Whatever additional strains sounded through his proclamation of the Gospel, his is never the voice of constraint. He waited for a "yes" from those to whom he spoke. Without this consent, the adherence he craved was valueless. This is decisive, and this is what gives his proclamation its historical stature.

Perhaps when the hope for a speedy success of his peaceful policy proved illusory, Constantine might have grown impatient and might then have considered quicker methods of obtaining his goal. The more he believed himself to be striving for the right desired by God, the more might he have been tempted to hasten the faltering course and assist the truth with the aid of the state. Constantine was clear, however, that such methods were not feasible and would violate the principles he had so solemnly proclaimed. Whether or not patience would succeed he could not tell, because in human affairs there can be no assurance, but this he saw—that a course adopted on principle can be compromised by compulsion. Constantine gave no occasion for reproach. The tolerance he had proclaimed remained the basis of his policy.[5]

---

are to be distinguished? We have already called attention to the nontheological factors in sect formation. More than that was involved here.

5. The peculiar quality of Constantine's tolerance comes to light when it is compared with parallels. With regard to

But his son thought to further this policy by going a step beyond. He proceeded to forbid sacrifices and close temples.[6] To be sure, his program met with

Henry IV, who ended the French wars of religion through the Edict of Nantes, Morley, the biographer of Voltaire, has this to say: "Henry the Fourth was a hero with Voltaire, for no better reason than that he was the first great tolerant, the earliest historic indifferent" (*Voltaire, 3,* 144). To be sure, this statement oversimplifies the tolerance of Henry IV. He belonged to the so-called third party, which felt that only a few religious beliefs were essential and that Paris *vaut bien une messe.* But thereby the interests of the state were placed above those of religion and a doubt was expressed with regard to the traditional tables of the law. Thus, as a matter of fact, one of the elements in this tolerance was skepticism.

Even more was this so in the case of Frederick the Great. The famous statement that all religions must be tolerated and the government has only to see to it that none hurts the other, because each can be saved in his own way, served, as we well know, to protect the Catholic confessional schools and is on the same order as the tolerance of the Jesuit order in Prussia even after its dissolution by the pope. Whatever interest Frederick may have had in the survival of state-controlled churches, and whatever of Christian motives conscious or unconscious may have remained with him, his tolerance was not religiously motivated and was derived from interests of state without metaphysical reference.

6. A few years after the death of Constantine, the African Firmicus Maternus (between 343 and 350) sought with all the zeal of a convert to stir up not only his former coreligionists but also the young emperors Constans and Constantius to embark upon forcible measures against the old cult and its places of worship (*Julii Firmici Materni De errore profanarum religionum,* ed. Agostino Pastorino, Biblioteca di Studi Superiori, 27, Florence, 1955):

Modicum tantum superest ut legibus vestris funditus prostratus diabolus iaceat, ut extinctae idololatriae pereat funesta

49

little success, nor was it of long duration. He managed only to intensify the bitterness of his nephew and successor, Julian, who sharply repudiated his policy and returned to the abandoned altars of ancient Rome.

contagio, "Little remains but that the devil should be utterly prostrated by your laws" (20.7, line 93). Idololatriae excidium et profanarum aedium ruinam propitium Christi numen vestris manibus reservavit, "Christ has committed to your hands the extirpation of idolatry and the destruction of the profane temples" (line 107). Like Constantine, Firmicus Maternus speaks of the dragon, the god of many forms, standing behind the heathen cult (21.2, line 12: deus multiformis; ipse tortuosus draco). The costly idols should be turned into the mint and the temples should be assigned to the fiscus (28.6). Appeal was made to the mandates of Deuteronomy (13:6–10, c. 29.1), and for such thoroughgoing destruction of the heathen shrines the emperors were promised good fortune and success in their governance. In such a spirit the tract predicts: "Thus all will prove auspicious for you. You shall have victories, opulence, peace, plenty, health, triumphs, that under divine majesty you may govern the world in felicity": Sic vobis feliciter cuncta provenient, victoriae, opulentia, pax, copia, sanitas et triumphi, ut divina maiestate provecti, orbem terrae felici gubernetis imperio (29.4, line 65).

One almost feels that Augustine was warning against such a voice when he said in the first part of his great historical work, concluding with praises of the pious Emperor Theodosius, that eternal blessedness is indeed reserved for true piety, but all other things which maintain and exalt life—such as the world itself, light and air, earth, water and fruits, and the very soul, body, senses, reason, and life of man—are given equally to the good and to the bad. Included also was a great portion of that lordship exercised by the emperor (*De civitate Dei* 5.26, ed. Dombart, Teubner, Leipzig, 1863, p. 240, line 27). "One should indeed be a Christian for the sake of eternal life, but not in order to win the fortune of a Constantine" (25, p. 238, line 12).

Julian's short reign affords no full assurance as to his basic principles, especially since they appear to have been intensified in the course of their realization. This is evident, that he envisioned a pagan counterpart to the Constantinian Church and perhaps—though this cannot be conclusively demonstrated—his very tolerance was an ingredient in this counterpart. At any rate he who in other respects restored the policy of Diocletian declared that so far was he from forcing Christians to sacrifice that no Christian would be permitted to do so without prior purification. The Christian requirements for participation in the Lord's Supper were at this point carried over into the pagan cult, with a possibility also of influence from the mystery religions.

Julian's Christian successors reverted to the policy of Constantius with no greater impact or success.

The decisive step was taken by Theodosius. In the year 380 this emperor decreed: "We desire that all people governed by our clemency should live in accord with the religion which the Apostle Peter committed to the Romans and which he teaches to this day, as the faith affirms." [7] Although the law arose at the outset from a decision with regard to the Church, it was to dominate history at large for centuries to

7. *Codex Theodosianus*, 16.2.2. Cf. W. Ensslin, "Die Religionspolitik des Kaisers Theodosius d. Gr.," *Sitzungsberichte der Bayerischen Akademie der Wissenschaften, Philos.—hist. Kl.* (1953), Heft 2.

come. The Reformed Church of Zurich in the days of Ulrich Zwingli made this provision of the *Codex Theodosianus* the basis of the church-state relationship.[8] Both the Byzantine empire in the East and the Holy Roman Empire in the West found here the starting point for all their legislation concerning the churches, the heretics, and the heathen. From now on, there was to be but one religion for the empire. Whether the penalties were enforced or suspended, the basic question had been decided. The goal Constantine envisioned was to be achieved no longer in accord with his way of free persuasion but rather by enforcement through the arm of the state.

In this regard the empire returned to the presuppositions and policy of Diocletian. The affinity was actually great and can be pursued in detail. If one surveys the imperial legislation up to Justinian, one perceives the extent to which the Christian empire was linked to the pagan. To be sure, the reasons for the legislation were not often stated. Constantine was an exception also in this respect. But where reasons were assigned, they bear the stamp of Rome: "All that provokes God to wrath and hurts souls we desired banished from the hearing of men"; "He who goes astray in the divine religion commits a public crime because he injures all"; "Addiction to the error of the impious heathen and its practice provoke the just wrath of the merciful God." [9] Public calamity,

8. Cf. *Konstantin* (see below, Bib. Note), p. 142.
9. *Codex Justinianus*, ed. Paul Krueger (Berlin, 1877), 1.3

52

failure of harvest, and pestilence were considered punishments for heathen infidelity.[1] It was the duty of
the emperor to expiate and check godlessness in the
suppression of all alien cults. If one makes a comparison with the contemporary heathen arguments in
favor of the retention of the ancient cult as voiced by
two of the best-known representatives of the heathenism lately dispossessed—namely Libanius, the Greek
orator, and Symmachus, the senator of old Rome—
one observes at once the kinship, for they urged that
the fertility of the land and the certainty of harvests depended upon the continuance of the temples and the
ancient rites.[2]

---

(a.448): πάντα γὰρ τὰ κινοῦντα τὸν θεὸν εἰς ὀργὴν συγγράμματα
καὶ τὰς ψυχὰς ἀδικοῦντα οὐδὲ εἰς ἀκοὰς ἀνθρώπων ἐλθεῖν βουλόμεθα.
5.4 (a.407): Ac primum quidem volumus esse *publicum
crimen*, quia quod in religione divina committitur, in omnium
fertur iniuriam. 11.10: ἐπειδή τινες εὕρηνται τῇ τῶν ἀνοσίων καὶ
μυσαρῶν Ἑλλήνων κατεχόμενοι πλάνῃ κἀκεῖνα πράττοντες ἅπερ
εἰς δικαίαν ὀργὴν κινεῖ τὸν φιλάνθρωπον θεόν, οὐδὲ τὰ περὶ τούτων
ἀδιόρθωτα καταλιπεῖν ὑπέστημεν.

1. *Leges novellae ad Theodosianum pertinentes*, ed. T.
Mommsen and Paul M. Meyer (Berlin, 1905), Vol. 2, p. 10,
line 75; cf. *Selbstzeugnis*, p. 341.

2. Libanius, *Oratio pro templis* 9, 10. Symmachus, *Relatio*
3.16, *Mon. Germ. Hist. Auct. Antiqui*, 6, Pt. I (1883), p. 283,
lines 7–9. Arnobius (*Adversus nationes* 2.7; ed. Reifferscheid,
1875) replied to the complaints of the heathen that since the
advent of Christianity the earth had been less fruitful and
fortunate. He enumerated the charges in detail: the gods
aroused by the revilings of the Christians have sent pestilences,
droughts, wars, famines, locusts, mice, hail, and other noxious
ills: pestilentias, inquiunt, et siccitates, bella, frugum inopiam,
locustas, mures et grandines resque alias noxias, quibus negotia

53

At the same time, the intolerance of the imperial church of Theodosius is not to be regarded as a mere continuation of heathen intolerance, as if only the name had been altered. One would not properly appreciate the quality of the new were one not to find in it something peculiar to itself. Christian intolerance had a root of its own which struck much deeper than the heathen.

Pagan intolerance required that one attend a sacrifice or provide an oblation, but thoughts were left free. The Christian Church, on the other hand, gathered a congregation whose members had to participate in the worship with a deepened understanding of religion. The discharge of an official duty was not suffi-

incursantur humana, dii nobis important iniuriis uestris atque offensionibus exasperati (1.3; p. 5, line 19, cf. p. 6, line 7; and 1.13, p. 11, line 12: Christianorum, inquiunt, causa mala di ingerunt et interitus comparatur ab superis frugibus). Arnobius, to show that the complaints had more than a recent origin, not only pointed to the calamities that preceded the Christian era but claimed that actually things had grown better. Since the time of Christ, wars had not increased but rather had decreased, or at least had been mitigated in severity (1.6, p. 8, lines 3 ff.), and this Christian Roman added a reference also to the expansion of the empire (1.14, p. 11, lines 23 ff.). The unbroken survival of this ancient belief is demonstrated by a passage cited by E. C. Dewick (*The Christian Atitude to Other Religions*, Cambridge, Eng., 1953, p. 131) from a sermon preached before King John III of Portugal in 1665: "God says: 'O Kingdom of Portugal: I promise thee the restoration of all the kingdoms which once paid thee tribute, and the conquest of many other still wealthier ones, if thou wilt make them [the heathen] fall down and worship Me.'"

cient, for the whole personal life had to be dedicated to God. But now, when the state gave political sanction to Christianity and sought to disseminate it by political means, the jurisdiction of the state extended to souls and consciences. For that reason the intolerance of the Christian faith was more incisive and far-reaching. If counter forces had not arisen on Christian soil to demand inner freedom from all human authority, the outcome would have resembled the modern totalitarian states.

Christian intolerance cut deeper and was something other than a continuance of the religious attitude of Rome dressed in a Christian costume precisely because there was a specifically Christian root. The more the Christian faith attached salvation exclusively to Christ and the more the great commandment made the Christian responsible for the welfare of his neighbor—not only in physical but also in spiritual need—the more must the Christian feel himself obligated to recall the erring from the path of destruction. One had to do something about the faith of others even if those imperiled resisted the measures taken on their behalf. In this way Christian motives were grafted on to the pagan motives, invested them with a new life, and provided them with a good conscience.

For this reason it is by no means anomalous that precisely the most religious and conscientious rulers were the ones to establish and sharpen the intolerance of the Christian empire. Mindful of their responsibility as rulers, they were bound to leave no means untried to bring all subjects from the path of error and to the way of truth. Constantine also desired this and recoiled only from the last step—civil constraint. As soon as his reserve was abandoned and men entertained illusions as to their power to coerce conformity, the ominous step was taken. The line ran from the wooing patience of the first Christian emperor to the state-church intolerance of that ruler who, while seeking to imitate Constantine, yet went far beyond him.

We no longer agree with Theodosius, but it would be unfair to see in the Byzantine and Western state churches nothing more than the obstinacy of an encrusted dogmatism conjoined with imperial absolutism to crush subjects by ruthless severity against body and soul. Were we to render such a judgment, we should make ourselves incapable of understanding how for centuries the noblest and most energetic spirits were sincerely committed to this view.

The most vocal example among the church fathers in the West was Augustine. He did not think in terms of the union of church and state, and there is little trace remaining in him of the old *Romanitas*. Opposed at first to any constraint in religion, he came to advocate it on the basis of his own experience. The arguments he adduced in favor of civil laws governing religion have since been interminably repeated. He forged the weapon with which the Medieval Church justified its procedure. His word moved Christian princes to do with greater zeal that to which they were in any case inclined.

At first Augustine had reservations about invoking the aid of the state against the schismatic church in Northern Africa, and he compelled the bishops in his diocese to exercise a like restraint, but when the emperor, unsolicited, stepped in and his forcible measures proved effective, Augustine changed his mind.

Particularly noteworthy are the reasons adduced by Augustine for his change of conviction. "My original opinion was that no one can be compelled to the unity of Christ. We should work only with the word, fight with disputations and conquer by reasonings, lest open heretics be turned into feigned Catholics." [3] At the outset he reproached a Donatist for forcing a servant to come into the Donatist Church.[4] An unwilling confession is worthless.[5] Previously he had warned: "One should not ask the emperor for punitive legislation against the heretics"; "We do not desire that the sufferings of the servants of God be requited by like measures"; "No one should be compelled to the Catholic truth, lest we have false and insincere Catholics." [6] This persuasion governed Augustine's conduct up to 404. Then, when there was talk of applying to the Donatists the law of Theodosius which imposed fines on the clergy of the heretics, Augustine instigated an episcopal delegation to the court to petition that the

3. *Ep.* 93.17; *CSEL* 34, p. 461, line 22.
4. *Ep.* 66.2; *CSEL* 34, p. 236.
5. *Ep.* 35.4; *CSEL* 34, p. 30.
6. *Epistulae* 185.13.19–21, *Corpus Scriptorum Ecclesiasticorum Latinorum* 57, p. 12.

law be applied only if violence had been used. The bishops desired of the state only that the Catholic truth may be freely taught and held; no one should be compelled to it "lest we have hypocritical Catholics." [7] But when news of Donatist outrages prompted the emperor to more severe action, Augustine gradually changed his opinion. Particularly the success of this policy impressed him. "It was not words but examples which changed my mind." [8] Among these examples his own city held first place. Whereas before it had been prevailingly Donatist, now so many had come over through fear of the imperial laws that the town was as Catholic as once it had been schismatic.[1] The same had happened in many other towns, which now sharply repudiated the schism and loved unity.[2] Thus it had been "the great mercy of God" which impelled the emperor to severity.[3]

Now he said: "Hypocritical adherence makes possible at least instruction by the Church"; "How can a Christian ruler serve God unless by impeding that which is contrary to God's command? Is one allowed to say to such a ruler: 'You have no business to concern yourself with attacks on your Lord, nor with His defense'? The kings in the Old Testament were praised because they rooted out the abominations. The hand of God Himself is working through the Christian em-

7. *Ep.* 185.25; *CSEL* 57, p. 24, line 20.
8. *Ep.* 93.17; *CSEL* 34, p. 461, line 26.
1. Ibid., p. 462, line 1.
2. *Ep.* 93.16; *CSEL* 14, p. 461, line 11.
3. *dei maior misericordia: Ep.* 185.26; *CSEL* 57, p. 25, line 3.

perors." "There is also a just persecution, that of love, which summons from error to the truth, in order to redeem its enemies from corruption." "Of course instruction is to be preferred to punishment." "Better is it when love leads, but many have to be brought in first by fear. For this reason the compulsory laws are a benefit to those constrained, as they will themselves eventually recognize even if not at first." Only—the penalty should not touch body and life. Here Augustine recoiled from the means later used by the Medieval Church. He did consider fines and banishment as permissible and advisable.[9]

From now on, Augustine began to justify coercion. What is right for one must in the end be fair for another. "Why should not the Church compel her lost sons to return when they compel others to go under?" [10] Then force was justified on biblical grounds. Paul was forcibly converted by Christ, and the Church only imitated her Lord in converting the Donatists.[1] The famous exposition of *coge intrare* in Luke 14:23, which turns a friendly invitation into a forcible induction, shows how hard pressed the exegete was to find a biblical text conformable to his experience. The real justification was the experience that

9. For Augustine on religious liberty consult Roland H. Bainton, *Castellio* (New York, 1935) and Lorenz, *Theologische Rundschau*, new ser. *25* (1929), 29. On the preference for Theodosius cf. Beza, *Tract. Theol.*, *1* (Geneva, 1570), 141.

10. *Ep.* 185.23; *CSEL* 57, p. 21, line 17.

1. *CSEL* 57, p. 22, line 19.

civil constraint could break the resistance not only of the outward but also of the inward man. The voluntary testimony of those converted through constraint silenced all earlier reservation.

To be sure, his surrender was not without qualification, inasmuch as he insisted on purity of motive and on love as the prime concern toward those constrained, that they might be saved against their will. He requested mild treatment even for the violent Circumcellions. They should not be touched in body and life. The Catholic bishops should suffer themselves to be killed rather than engage in executions: etiam occidi ab eis eligamus, quam eos occidendos vestris iudiciis ingeramus.[2]

Augustine was candid enough not to throw upon the state the full responsibility for the force used on behalf of the Church. She carries the onus. But he committed himself to the dubious proposition that the end justifies the means: "If those in the highways and byways—that is, in heresy and schism—are forced by the power in due time conferred by God through the rulers upon the Church, those affected should not complain that they are compelled, but should attend to that to which they are compelled." (Si potestate, quam per religionem ac fidem regum tempore, quo debuit, diuino munere accepit ecclesia, hi, qui inveniuntur in uiis et in saepibus, id est in haeresibus et

2. *Ep.* 100; *CSEL* 34, p. 537, line 17; cf. *Ep.* 134.4, *CSEL* 44, p. 87, line 9; *Ep.* 133, *CSEL* 44, p. 81, line 15; and *Ep.* 139.2, *CSEL* 44, p. 150.

schismatibus, coguntur intrare, non, quia coguntur, reprehendant, sed, quo cogantur, adtendant.) [3]

Augustine describes the inner working of the constraint which breaks down obstinacy and opens the door to truth. This will not create the good, which both after and before has to be voluntary, but does create the indispensable condition for it: Non quo quisque bonus esse possit inuitus, sed timendo quod non uult, pati uel relinquit impedientem animositatem uel ignoratam compellitur cognoscere ueritatem, ut timens uel respuat falsum de quo contendebat uel quaerat uerum, quod nesciebat et uolens iam teneat quod nolebat.[4]

But experience is an inadequate teacher. Even the most far-seeing eye, standing on the highest pinnacle, can scan only the immediate results of human deeds, and fails to discern the effects upon those who suffer constraint, those who exercise it, and those who witness it. From the point of view of the essential core of the Christian faith, one can wish that Augustine had stayed true to his own conviction. Unhappily he ceased to rely on the power of the simple word and trusted to the quicker and more evident thrust of the civil sword.

Augustine's model Christian emperor was not so much Constantine as Theodosius, whose piety was evident not only in his personal humility but also in his measures against everything heathen. "Throughout

3. *Ep.* 185.24; *CSEL* 57, p. 23, line 16.
4. *Ep.* 93.16; *CSEL* 34, p. 461, line 5.

the empire he ordered the destruction of pagan statues because he well knew that even earthly blessings are the gift not of demons but of the true God." [5]

Ignaz Döllinger, the renowned Catholic Church historian, associates the shift in the Church's position on constraint in religion with Augustine. This shift, says Döllinger, "may indeed be regarded as a defection from the ancient teaching: he assumes that the emperors were the teachers of the bishops." [9]

Augustine, surprised by the success of the state's compulsory measures, made them the basis of theses of the greatest importance. The Biblical support for which he looked he himself had to improvise by means of an artificial exegesis: the New Testament afforded no help. It is astonishing how much closer the Emperor Constantine came to the New Testament at this point than did the great theologian. To be sure, Constantine's own past urged him to hold liberty in high esteem: he had struggled for it and his experience confirmed his evaluation. Augustine, on the other hand, had experienced the power of grace breaking his self-will, and he had known the blessing of being conquered by redemption. The statesman easily understood the de-

5. [Theodosius I]: simulacra gentilium ubique evertenda praecepit, satis intelligens nec terrena munera in daemoniorum, sed in Dei veri esse posita potestate (Augustine, *De civitate Dei* 5.26, ed. Dombart, p. 240, line 13). Augustine combines the measures against the idols directly with the measures against heresy: Inter haec omnia [the wars of the usurpers] ex ipso initio imperii sui non quievit iustissimis et misericordissimis legibus adversus impios laboranti ecclesiae subvenire (line 8).

9. *Akademische Vorträge*, 3 (1891), 277 f.

mand of political wisdom which commended sparing the old Roman cult to which the majority of his subjects still adhered. The bishop lived in the Theodosian empire, which abrogated the rights of the temple, and he was under the impression that the provision for compulsory entry into the Church was really an act of benevolence; the two men were motivated by opposing experiences.

Beyond that fact it is certain that Constantine chose to be the advocate of a position whose spokesman had hitherto been the Christian Church, while Augustine surrendered the better insight that he himself had formerly represented. His rich, more profound, Christian understanding was at this point eclipsed by the sure instinct for the right to which Constantine's Edict of Toleration gave voice. Here the emperor grasped the Christian faith while the Christian theologian slipped unawares into the religious attitude of antiquity.

The merciful severity which would restrain the erring even against his will from destruction remained the basis for the legal action of the Christian state for more than a thousand years. Medieval intolerance was derived both from classical and from Christian sources. Curiously the objection to it had also these two roots. Libanius, whose plea for the pagans we have noticed, used Christian arguments.[10] "In the law of the Christians themselves," said he, "persuasion is commended and constraint condemned." "Why do you rage against the temples and thus transgress your

10. Cf. above, p. 53.

own laws?" "In such matters one must persuade, not compel. He who cannot do the first and reverts to the second does not succeed but deceives himself."[1] These are considerations first adduced by Christians against heathen emperors, now addressed to a Christian emperor with full awareness that they are primitive Christian assumptions. But he to whom the eloquent defender of the pagan shrines appealed by name was Constantine. However much Libanius complained that the first Christian emperor had ceased to sacrifice and was using temple funds to construct his city, he praised Constantine because he left the temples intact and permitted the ancient rites to continue. At the end of this period, which thought to bring Constantine's work to completion, his tolerance of the pagans was once more expressed. But it was not proclaimed by Theodosius, who aspired to be united in heaven with Constantine and believed that he was implementing his policy on earth.[2] Rather, those who entered these pleas were the advocates of paganism. The quality of Constantine becomes fully apparent only when one sees him as the pivotal figure of a great hour in history standing between two eras of which the second thought to follow him and adopted his name.

An hour of history—it was an hour constituted by a transforming deed, an insight into the spiritual significance of the event and a moral decision. One would

1. *Oratio pro templis* 20.
2. Ambrosius, *De obitu Theodosii* 40.

scarcely employ the expression "an hour of history" to brilliant discoveries by individuals nor even to catastrophes affecting whole peoples, no matter how great their import or how far-reaching their impact. Such an hour and no mere episode speaks to us, and our readiness to listen betokens its greatness.

Still, only after history has been investigated in its own context will it turn its face toward us. An hour or a figure of the past must be measured and grasped in its own place before it can meet us. It must be seen as a whole, else we are lost in details. Much in the past appears to us akin and thereby diminishes our sense of distance. Other matters, which at first appear remote, are actually closer and can disclose themselves to us. But in either case full account must be taken of the entire situation as it then was. If the past is to speak to our condition, artificially interpolated questions and comparisons must remain without an answer. Against any hasty attempts to apply scholarship to life, Leopold Ranke entered a protest when he said, "We can exercise a genuine effect on the present only when we first turn away from it and dedicate ourselves to free objective research." [3] Not until we have fully confronted the past do we discern its unexpected depth, and in this confrontation we attain a surer understanding of ourselves. It may even be that no contemporary can speak to us with such compelling power. The answer to which we feel ourselves driven by historical investigation tells us more about our-

3. *Historische Zeitschrift*, 27, 143.

selves than ever we knew. Such an encounter with the past may lead to a self-knowledge never experienced by one who is the prisoner of the present.

In confrontation with an hour of history there is a dialogue of question and answer in which understanding acquires new dimensions. We approach the past with our questions and imperceptibly the past poses questions for us.

Before our eyes the emperor begins to explain his way, and we feel ourselves summoned in dialogue with him to justify our way, or to alter it, since we do not regard our way as forever prescribed and fixed.

Constantine, we recall, claimed to have ended the old intolerance without erecting another. He could not conceal his own conviction—that he made plain —he had to confess the truth as it declared itself to him, and he had to brand error as error, but at the same time he had to allow error free course—and not simply because error might contain a grain of truth, nor because he needed the aid of the erring; such tolerance would have lasted only so long as these grounds continued to be valid. Rather, he held that truth itself demanded tolerance. This provided a sure footing to tolerance and at the same time the recognition that it is a means rather than an end. Its meaning is not to be found in itself; yet as tolerance adheres to the truth, like truth it becomes unassailable. In such truth freedom addresses itself to man—this must not be overlooked. He is called to right use of freedom and he perverts the meaning of freedom by misuse. Freedom does not prevent misuse, but man must know that in the misuse he abuses himself.

This is what Constantine has to say to us. These are the thoughts he associated with the religious liberty he had proclaimed. One who views them from the present receives a divided impression. Some elements attract and others repel. Both the strangeness and the familiarity warn against accepting this impression without qualification. Perhaps modern tolerance herself has now to address her questions to the emperor. She must then reflect upon his answers.

To us it seems strange and inconsistent that the emperor should at the same time extend toleration and condemn those to whom it was granted. How could he so flatly reject the upright and often earnest faith of his pagan subjects? Did they not have on their side much that had made Rome great and venerable: loyalty to the ancestral altars and proud love for the empire—whereas the Christians hitherto not only had been held aloof but had themselves deliberately stood aloof? Yet Constantine's tolerance contributed something which at no time has been self-evident. He held fast to his policy with no gain from the pagan side and even in the full knowledge that the state was thereby exposed to danger. This meant that he could not be disillusioned in his expectations and induced in consequence to revoke toleration. His was not an unreflective opportunistic tolerance which veers according to circumstance. His combination of tolerance and disapproval ensured tolerance against reversal. His answer throws the question back to us as to how firmly our own tolerance is grounded.

The first question posed by modern tolerance to the emperor has arisen out of our confident assumption that we have gone beyond him. The second question is derived, however, from our uncertainty, and betrays the crisis of tolerance in our time. And if in the first instance she asked whether he had not gone too far, now she inquires whether he has gone far enough.

Constantine was persuaded that the pagan cult was devoted to demonic powers. That meant that its devotees endangered not only themselves but also the empire. To be sure, Constantine was not afraid that the religious opposition would stage a revolution and set up a pagan counterempire. His throne was sufficiently well established to have no concern on that score, and the pagans actually did not entertain any such plans. The danger was of another sort. Constantine interpreted his victory as a divine judgment on the pagan gods—but could he stop there? If he was further convinced that the religious unity of the empire and the continuance of divine favor belonged together, did not the continuance of the pagan temples imperil both? And was he not responsible? Why then did he not suppress the temples?

The question brings to light difficulties in our own position. Of course sacrifice and temple worship no longer appear to us to be dangerous but our generation is confronted by other dangers which cause us to

68

waver in our tolerance. We are faced by a power struggle between comprehensive political philosophies making absolute claims for their doctrines of salvation. As they grant no tolerance, so they look upon tolerance as proof of decadence. What is tolerance to do in the face of such claims? Shall she leave the preachers of this teaching unrestricted and thereby open the door to her own undoing? An answer here presents itself which at first glance appears to be satisfactory, namely that tolerance cannot tolerate intolerance. He who denies tolerance cannot ask for it. Such a solution does not however resolve the difficulty but rather brings it all the more to light, because if intolerance is to be paid back in the same coin, then the intolerance of every period can drive tolerance to renounce itself and become on its own part intolerant. In that case its own existence depends upon how much latitude is allowed by intolerance.

But still more dangerous is the transformation to which tolerance is exposed, because in the rejection of the intolerant ideology there is unwittingly built up a counterdoctrine which comes to resemble that of the opponent. One passes over—hesitatingly at first, then ever more willingly—to the ground of the aggressor. Thus there develops out of tolerance a counterideology, which comes to have the same exclusive and coercive character as that to which it is opposed. This transmutation may be seen when in the name of tolerance one begins to spy out convictions to see if one can uncover the hidden roots of his opponents' teachings. All reservations are then canceled, and whatever deviates from the line is held suspect and worthy to be crushed, on the ground that it is too intolerant to be tolerated. Even though naked force is avoided, ways are found to fell the opponent most effectively by threats soft or loud, by pointing the finger, by insinuation, social ostracism, and the stirring up of popular passion. In the end, tolerance is interchangeable with intolerance.

Constantine found himself constrained to grant toleration to those who had been persecutors and whose position he deemed dangerous. He did so regardless of the warnings which came to him from friends and which were not foreign to his own thinking. What restrained him from following such voices was the command of his own faith to take seriously the freedom even of the erring. This enabled him to live with his own conscience.

Can his behavior say anything to us? Does this mean that one must grant liberty to any sincere conviction even when there is danger that by it we shall be engulfed? To this we should say no. But the word of Constantine means more than this. Because he looked upon freedom as a demand of faith he did not consider expediency, as if freedom had its price and circumstance would determine whether it should be upheld or denied.[4] In that case freedom would be only one value among others, perhaps a very great value but

4. Intolerance is not overcome exclusively by better insight. Often enough it is overcome by arguments that in the scales have more weight than words. In the time of the ancient Church many congregations brought considerable sums to

70

nevertheless one that might be superseded, however regretfully it were relinquished. Constantine points us to a much deeper ground of freedom.

If we accept his directive, it will still be true that force must be repelled by force, but we shall not deny respect to those who think differently. We shall guard their freedom because only in this way can truth and faith be won. He who holds a position of responsibility in the state is called upon to observe these limits. He must see to it that no group trespasses upon another, not even the group with which he agrees. He must also see to it that the state uses none of the means at its disposal to restrict or suppress convictions. Thus from out of the remote past the first Byzantine emperor reminds the modern religiously neutral state that it can be protected by convinced faith from succumbing to an ideology by which it is itself destroyed.

But tolerance suffers not only from embarrassment as to what should be done with the intolerant, but also from uncertainty as to how to answer their objections, for they say that tolerance leads to indifference to

---

ransom threatened leaders, and many local officials looked through their fingers. So has it been throughout history up to the time when Jewish coreligionists in the time of Hitler sent dollars to ransom prisoners. Yet gold was not the only way to induce intolerance to release its victims. Influence, power, and political support have exerted considerable effect. Calvin mediated an alliance between King Francis I of France and the Protestant princes of the Schmalkald League on behalf of their French coreligionists, whose persecution might cease if the German allied troops were to be spared the sight of burning scaffolds. Cromwell interceded effectively for the Waldenses and the Huguenots.

truth and unconcern for men.[1] Intolerance claims to speak in the name of truth and undertakes by force to bring men to the truth.[2]

Constantine's judgment on the heathen appears to be an expression of intolerance, but it is of another quality. The rejection applied not to the men but to their error. Though the emperor was persuaded that he spoke in the name of truth, he was not minded to constrain anyone to accept it. To be sure, truth and a belief that life depends upon truth conditioned his approach to the erring. But even the truth—contrary to the opinion of the sixteenth-century inquisitor or the twentieth-century totalitarian—requires a *yes* freely spoken. In this she discloses her nature, which is very different

1. The article by Ernest W. Nelson, "The Theory of Persecution," in *Persecution and Liberty. Essays in Honor of George Lincoln Burr* (New York, 1931), pp. 3–20, confines itself to the theory of "corporal punishment for heresy in Christendom," but it would be profitable to pursue the theory of "saving constraint."

2. M. Searle Bates, *Religious Liberty: An Inquiry* (New York, 1945), quotes from a modern encyclopedia the statement: "Intolerance is of the essence of every church, an immediate consequence of its faith that it possesses the only effective means for the salvation of the soul" (*Encyclopedia of the Social Sciences, 13*, 239–46). This statement gives occasion to the reproach that tolerance fosters indifference. Cf. the word of John Stuart Mill: "Religious Liberty has hardly anywhere been practically realized, except where religious indifference, which dislikes to have its peace disturbed by theological quarrels, has added its weight to the scale." Still more radical is the thesis of Francesco Ruffini, who held that "the idea of a single and universal God" entails

72

from the inhuman dogma that "shuts the gates of mercy on mankind." As tolerance here displaces intolerance, she must pass judgment because she is bound to truth, yet she must allow freedom because she rests upon persuasion. Truth is concerned for the man and therefore cannot leave him to himself to go his own way, and the less so when his error imperils not only himself but also the commonweal. For this reason Constantine, and the Christians who listened to him, derived from the severity of the judgment a directive to seek out the heathen. Against any intimidation stood the fundamental principle that faith cannot be intimidated. The pagan was shielded by a respect for freedom. The responsible tolerance of Constantine permitted the pagan to go his own way, yet did not suffer him simply to withdraw. There was room within this tolerance for contests of the spirit conjoined with peace among the contestants.

Constantine thus can help tolerance to forfend the

---

a thoroughgoing intolerance: "From this followed not only an inextinguishable spirit of proselytism but also the principle that he only could be saved who worshipped the true God, that is to say, the principle of absolute intolerance" (*Religious Liberty*, London, 1912, p. 19). Heinrich Bornkamm well observes that "because the Reformation did not find the way to tolerance out of faith, there came about tolerance out of unbelief" (*Historikerkongress*, 1958; cf. his essay "Glaube und Toleranz," *Deutsche Zeitung*, 8, No. 6, 1957, p. 4). Cf. a philosophical insight of our own day: "Only in dedication to truth can freedom be fulfilled." "A merely formal freedom is easily perverted" (Karl Jaspers, *Wahrheit, Freiheit und Friede*, 1958, pp. 12–13).

objections of intolerance. The intolerant by their very behavior refute the pretention to speak in the name of truth. The force they use can only beget in man a disregard for truth. If, as they say, they are concerned for the man, nevertheless by what they do they crush the man. The intolerant have no right to their objections not only because they fail in their objective but also because by their method they are all the more certain to fail.

Tolerance found in Constantine a notable champion. But he who became her advocate, and rejected intolerance, after a while began unawares to question tolerance. He desired a tolerance which speaks to the erring. Is a mere permissiveness, which keeps silent, of the same quality? He drew near to those who were tolerated even when he passed upon them a sharp judgment. Would holding aloof from them have been a more humane mode of behavior? He who would answer negatively is bound to say what is truth and what is error. He who shrinks from doing so and regards such judgments as arrogant is not thereby extricated from the situation. His very silence speaks and shows that judgment has already been passed and indicates what it is. When Constantine saw that truth was not with intolerance, it might seem that simply to oppose intolerance made him the champion of truth. But the way in which he combined truth and freedom shows that the matter is not so simple. The ally which tolerance had found in him compelled her to make discriminating distinctions. Neither unqualified rejection nor recognition was possible. An unequivocal judgment of condemnation is not violence, and nonviolence as such is not tolerance.

In our own day the coining and use of the word intolerance show the need for more precise definition.[3] The attack on intolerance belongs to modern times. The word was coined to describe those who reject what was deemed to be the higher worth of tolerance. When general approval had been attained for wresting confessional freedom from the confessional state, men took heart for the next step of digging after the root

3. If tentatively one draws lines connecting points, the direction of the development appears to fall into three periods. The first, in which the word "tolerance" acquires its new meaning, is the one in which the demand for tolerance is directed more to the state than to the church. However much the ruler may be surrounded by jurists and theologians and however much he may accept the medieval picture of the state in harmony with and directed by the church, the appeal is directed to the prince and not to the bishop. In the second period, after the wars of religion, tolerance, having grown more assured and broader in her pretentions, turned against the church and now branded the opponent with the polemical word "intolerant." The authority denied to the church was transferred to the state, even though the state did not become heir also to the church's claim to truth. In the last period, tolerance has entered the area of the private. The question now is with regard to the attitude and mood of the individual. The duty of tolerance seems to be bound up with the social existence of men, even though they are not cognizant of the grounds. The grounds offered are varied—some disputable, some from direct evidence. But the question still remains how these demands are compatible with an unqualified claim to truth. On the answer depends the future of tolerance.

of the evil, which was taken to be clerical domination and the doctrinal rigidity that makes heretics of others. Were not these the causes of the wars of religion? Down, then, with the dominance of the church and her coercive dogmas! The most convenient instrument for the dethronement of the church was the modern state. But in wielding this instrument, men came imperceptibly under its dominance. The *Leviathan* of Thomas Hobbes, on the threshold of the eighteenth century, portended ominously the totalitarian state of the twentieth century. He went so far as to expunge expressly the Christian reservation with regard to obedience to the state. In the first edition he contested the right of the so called *clausula Petri* (Acts 5:29), "We ought to obey God rather than man."

The case of Hobbes raises the question how far the attack of tolerance on intolerance touched the authority of the Christian Church. Was the objection to the breach of their commission by the commissioners or to the commission itself? Does our tolerance attack merely the system of sophisticated theology which superseded the original Christian message, or the very gospel itself? He who attacks the faith can perhaps say that its spokesmen have made the belief unbelievable; but if he rejects the belief, he has demolished the only basis on which a genuine tolerance can rest, and in his case the tolerance remaining has become inconsequential. Tolerance and intolerance to this day bear the marks of this dispute. Intolerance justifies itself on the ground that tolerance springs from enmity or indifference to religion. On the other hand "tolerance," from which comes "intolerance," [4] extends the meaning to the point of revelation. Tolerance has been so successful that even in scholarly parlance her terminology is regnant. The term thus originated by controversy has not been thought through. We assume that anything which is called intolerant is forthwith to be rejected without examination. Thus a designation which began as a weapon in history has passed over to the domain of logic, and seems now incontestable.

But then, too, the opponents of tolerance have taken the word over into their camp. Hitler and Lenin confessed to a fanatical intolerance. More amazing is the way in which Christian theologians speak lightly of the intolerance of revelation. They fail to see that the word, because of its derivation, carries the overtones of bitter contention. He who uses it adopts the presupposition of the enemy. We are no more able today than in the age of the Enlightenment to make a distinction, so far as the term goes, between Jesus and the Great Inquisitor, between the sublimity of the gospel and its monstrous perversion.

There are, then, three questions to be addressed to Constantine from the standpoint of modern tolerance. The first question, as to the reason for the strange combination of tolerance and rejection, receives the answer that tolerance is more firmly grounded when it

4. Contra R. Bultmann, *Das Evangelium des Johannes* (1957), p. 288.

has nothing to expect from those to whom it is directed.

The second question asks whether dangerous teachings can be tolerated. Here it must be remembered that in the conflict with an intolerant ideology tolerance runs the danger of a no less intolerant counterideology, with the result that tolerance is itself extinguished.

The third question seeks a reply to the reproach that tolerance is concerned neither with truth nor with man, but leads to indifference. Here Constantine recalled that truth demands freedom and that it is precisely truth which is concerned for men. But when truth is separated from intolerance, then indeed tolerance must ask on her part how far she has taken seriously both truth and men.

These questions and answers do not obliterate the distance in time and space that separates us from Constantine. Rather, by inviting comparison they point up the difference and the peculiarity of each age. Such comparison denies the attempt to bring both times within one common and general evaluation which would not do justice to the difference of the conditions under which each age must act. The comparison necessitates our asking just what are the demands and the possibilities posed by each age for those who have to act within it. In this way the past is evaluated with sympathetic understanding and the present is illumined. Now the present becomes conscious of its historical situation and thus of its uniqueness. Only in such self-recognition is it able to grasp the task specifically put to it. Thus the general judgments that are made without differentiation about times and deeds far apart prove to have no sense of reality; indeed, when they strive to put their own age under the impact of nontemporal norms, they are dangerous and an enemy to life. On the other hand if we open ourselves toward another age and face its questions, we shall come to know ourselves, and such a confrontation will enable us to make judgments that will actually arrive at particular realities. Far from being a relativization bent on the dissolution of all that is definite and designed to make our feet slip, this confrontation permits judgments that are relevant and thus valid. If the past is understood, the present is also grasped, and a grasp of the present leads to intelligent action. Here we might stop and trust to the steady power of the picture itself that we have gained by looking into the distant past.[5]

5. Cf. Reinhard Wittram, *Das Interesse an der Geschichte* (Göttingen, 1958), p. 120: "The vivid realization of a past situation is not all that history can give us, but is perhaps her most precious and intimate offering."

# 2. Constantine and the Heretics

RELIGIOUS FREEDOM establishes no frontiers in the areas where it is proclaimed. We have dealt with the first Christian emperor's tolerance of the heathen. It now remains to consider his attitude to the dissident Christian groups. We must find out if it is, as we should expect, a valid test for our estimate of what we called Constantine's hour of history. Are the two problems homogeneous and therefore comparable in the light of that day's historical actuality? A hint that they may not be lies in the fact we can now no longer deal with events as they are forged into expression in individual documents. Instead we must trace a series of happenings by recounting them. So even the manner of treatment must be different from that of our original topic.

The laws relating to the heathen and the heretics since Theodosius belong very closely together. They proceed from the same principles and draw the same conclusions. Constantine's contemporaries had grouped the heathen and the heretics together. Athanasius asked why the Arians did not reckon themselves as heathens when they, too, talked about an ingenerate and a generate god, just as the heathen spoke of an uncreated god and many created gods. Constantine himself considered that the Donatists, when they appealed to the emperor against the judgments of the Church, ranked themselves with the heathen. And behind both he saw the same demonic power which they served and which conspired in all their deeds and endeavors. Our expectation that the guiding principles of Constantine's attitude toward the heathen should also be applied to the heretics therefore is not without support in the thought of that era itself. But what did the actual course of events turn out to be?

Constantine's first encounter with a schismatic group came in the West. The Donatist question plagued him to the end of his life, for he never found a complete solution.[1] Basic decisions were not lacking, but though they followed the order of events they were not opportunistic.

After the persecution came to an end, a controversy with regard to the replacement of the bishop arose in Carthage and speedily took on wider proportions. All along, there had been stricter and milder leanings. During the persecution the truculent and the discreet were not of one mind as to the proper course. A provocative

1. On the history of Donatism consult in particular W. H. C. Frend, *The Donatist Church* (Oxford, 1952), and the *Reallexikon für Antike und Christentum, 4,* 128–47, as well as B. H. Watmington, *The North African Provinces from Diocletian to the Vandal Conquest,* Cambridge, 1954. For the documents see *Urkunden zur Entstehung des Donatismus,* ed. H. Soden and H. Campenhausen (2d ed. Berlin, 1950), "Kleine Texte," No. 122.

attitude on the one hand and a craven caution on the other were alike rejected. Should Christians go in crowds to the prisons to visit the confessors and thus attract unfavorable attention to the congregation? On the other hand, should the imprisoned be left without the comfort and care of the brethren? When, then, Caecilian, the representative of the party of caution, was somewhat hastily elevated to the bishopric, certain malcontents, together with a number of Numidian bishops, assembled and installed a counterbishop. Speedily, definite parties crystallized, in which principles and personal grievances were inextricably combined. The eventual spokesman of the opposition was a determined man of no mean endowment, Donatus of Casae Nigrae, who gave his name to the movement. Only gradually did the points of division become clear.

Yet at the outset the basic cleavage was plain and centered on different views as to the meaning and role of the Church. The Donatists held fast to the remembrance of the Church as a community of saints which could not tolerate in its midst any major sins and certainly not denial of the faith. As early as the middle of the third century Bishop Cyprian of Carthage had relaxed enough so that he would not exclude indefinitely from the Church those who had lapsed in the persecution of Decius. But he preserved the ancient rigor with reference to the officers of the Church. The acts they had to perform called for purity on their part. This ground the Donatists would not yield. He who had denied the Lord could not celebrate the Lord's

Supper, baptize, or consecrate. All the official acts of the lapsed clergy were invalid. This position was of great significance for the way the Church conceived of herself. Cyprian had looked upon the bishops as the indispensable pillars of the Church. Was it of no consequence for their office if they failed in the hour of testing? The Donatists gave to this question a negative answer. When now the charge was made that the new bishop of Carthage had been consecrated by a man who in the persecution had surrendered the Sacred Scripture, his ordination was in their eyes invalid and his title untenable.

This controversy within the Church of necessity came to the attention of the civil authorities when they undertook to administer the Edict of Restitution of Church Property and the distribution of other favors conferred by Constantine upon the Church. If a congregation split, which group should be the recipient? The attitudes of the state could not long remain unaffected by the fact that the schism in the Church coalesced with fissures in the political and social structure. The non-Roman element in the population, particulary the Berbers, sought to assert themselves against the Roman upper class. Social revolutionaries formed fanatical fighting units called Circumcellions. Even in the fifth century they still sallied out on thundering expeditions, burning the villas of the Roman landlords and demolishing the Catholic churches. The strands were so interwoven and confused that to this day it is hard to tell whether the difference in dogma was the

84

occasion, the driving power, or merely the accompaniment of the political and social convulsions.[2] Enough that the two were inseparable and together prevented any rapprochement with the Catholic party, which was also the party of the Roman aristocracy. The measures taken by the government, alternately indulgent and repressive, served only to intensify the rifts, which in their turn were not without repercussions.

At the outset the behavior of the officials was correct and not precipitant. The proconsul properly informed the emperor that "certain persons," accompanied by a crowd, had appeared before him and deposed against Caecilian. "They handed me a sealed letter in leather of Cordova and a petition," to be transmitted to the court. The Donatist bishops were requesting the emperor to appoint judges to decide the case. They added that these might come from Gaul, where there had been no persecution and consequently no cases of apostasy. Constantine promised to appoint them. The controversy seemed to him concerned with "the observance of the churches' law" and whether the accused Bishop Caecilian was worthy to perform the rites of the Church. The emperor sent three Gallic bishops to Rome to investigate the complaint in conjunction with the Roman bishop. Caecilian should come to

2. After all, we must not forget that in the debates between the churches reference was made only to dogmatics and to those historical questions of importance for the concept of the Church, which leaves open the possibility of underlying unexpressed motives. Only those expressed were determinative.

Rome with ten bishops of his party and the Donatists should also be represented by ten.[3]

The decision went against Donatus, however indulgently his followers were treated. Yet they complained to the emperor that they had not been properly heard and that the judgment was not well founded. This was the reason for summoning the Council of Arles, to which the emperor invited the bishops of his entire domain. The synod confirmed the Roman decision, with a sharper rejection of unfounded claims. Only he whose guilt could be proved out of public documents and not through mere denunciation should be deposed from his office. False accusers were to be excluded from the Church. On the other hand, the official acts of apostates were valid. Those whom they had consecrated, if worthy, remained in office even though those who ordained them were themselves deposed.

These decisions were in line with the view Rome had held against Cyprian but which only now acquired universal recognition. From this point on, the validity of the official act of a Church officer was held not to depend on the worthiness of the person performing the act. The office itself would be deprived of all meaning if all baptized persons were fearful that some later discovery of a hidden sin on the part of the one

3. The view—sponsored in particular by Erich Caspar, *Geschichte des Papsttums*, 2 vols. Tübingen, 1930–33—that the bishop of Rome turned the civil commission into a Church council in order to ensure the independence of the Church is contested by U. Instinsky in his *Bischofstuhl und Kaiserthron*, Munich, 1955.

administering baptism were to invalidate the rite. If the efficacy of the office depended on the purity of the person, how could there be any assurance? Of course the Catholics also held that the unworthy should not become or remain priests. Proved guilt brought deposition. The clergyman was not a mere cultic functionary, but so long as a bishop or a priest exercised his office, the congregation should be assured that the sacraments he dispensed were the vehicles of salvation.

But for the Donatists the apostate had excluded himself from the ark of the Lord. Whatever he performed from then on was without efficacy. For Catholic teaching the office and the person were so far distinguished that the failure of the person was not the failure of the office. The African Church, which rallied around Caecilian, was compelled now by the synod to give up the practice prevalent in Africa since Cyprian, but not elsewhere in the empire, of rebaptizing heretics who came over to orthodoxy. Thus the anti-Donatist Church in Africa came into full alliance with the Catholic Church throughout the world.

But again, after Arles, the condemned appealed to the emperor. After some hesitation, he agreed to receive the appellants at his court and to render judgment himself. To be sure the decision had to wait some time, not simply because political problems demanded the emperor's attention but also because he first sent two bishops to Carthage with a compromise proposal. But their attempt, instead of uniting the parties under a mediating bishop, was wrecked by the opposition of both groups. There was now no further possibility of a reconciliation, and nothing was left but to live out the controversy. Constantine made a final gesture when he told the Donatists that if they could establish one single charge against Caecilian, he would concede their entire case.[4]

This is the background of a situation in which Constantine had to make his decision. One might assume that he acted from prejudice, because in accord with the advice of his clerical counselor, Bishop Ossius of Cordova, he conferred the advantages decreed by the state upon one side only. But when the other side appealed to him, he complied with the request of the Donatists and entrusted the case to the Gallic bishops in conjunction with the incumbent of the most outstanding see. He gathered representatives of the entire Western Church at the council and provided an opportunity for the first time to discuss in common the question at issue: that the unity of the Church be restored. He was all the more disturbed when the appellant bishops rejected the decision of the synod in which both the emperor and the Church believed Christ Himself to be present. To behave in this fashion was to repudiate the law of the Church and to act like heathen.[5] But however shocked he might be by their rejection of the Christian way proposed he would not brush aside their legal claim, and in accord with the provisions of the civil law himself investigated their

4. *Urkunden* (above, n. 1), No. 21.
5. Ibid., No. 18, pp. 24, 26.

accusations against the Bishop of Carthage. The verdict was that the accused bishop "had fulfilled the duties of his religion and discharged them fittingly." [6] Investigations in Africa disclosed the falsehood of the accusation that Caecilian had been ordained by an apostate. Inasmuch as every complaint had proved untenable, the emperor rejected the appeal and decided in favor of the accused.

Up to this point the question of tolerance had not been seriously raised. Nor could one properly speak of interference on the part of the emperor in the affairs of the Church, especially since his attempt at mediation was wrecked by the refusal of both parties. The breach could no longer be closed and a neutral solution was no longer available. There was nothing left but to let the law take its course.

But this meant that new measures had to be devised and enforced to meet the growing popular movement. The Donatists believed no less than ever that they were right and their opponents wrong. To be sure, the particular accusations they kept bringing up did not stand investigation. The Council of Arles had done well to accept only the evidence of official documents in order to dispel the dust cloud of suspicion and recrimination that hung over the field of battle. The emperor also would do no other than follow the course indicated by the appellants themselves. He must deal with the demonstrable facts. But the Donatists still did not feel that they had been properly refuted. The official acts

6. Ibid., p. 25.

on which the Council of Arles and Constantine relied were the acts of the Roman officials during the period of the persecution, and in the eyes of the Donatists they were not of any great value. The prudential caution that Caecilian had exercised during the persecution seemed to them little short of apostasy. The sign and the proof of true Christian faith they saw only in unintimidated steadfastness against a government which sought to break their firm confession. The situation was not greatly altered in their eyes because the emperor instead of requiring pagan sacrifice demanded submission to a politically subservient ecclesiastical domination.

A difference of conviction as to the faith rather than political or social considerations accounts for their irreconcilable attitude. To be sure, popular passions had contributed to their resistance, and they may have been partly to blame for the confusion of the issue, but their opponents did not help them in the least at this point. When the Donatists declined to give up some of the churches in Carthage that had been assigned to the Catholics, Caecilian appealed to the government. The ruthless use of force by the military, composed in part of pagans, ruptured definitely the bond of brotherhood.[7]

The Donatists regarded themselves as constituting

7. On the events in Carthage consult Frend, pp. 159 ff. With regard to the extension of the persecution—that is, the banishment of the bishops—here, too, the numbers involved appear to have been small.

the Church of the martyrs. Just as martyrdom had once been the end of Christian endeavor, so now the Donatist martyrs were held in great and even in extravagant esteem. Even before the schism this was a point of contention. There had been resentment against Caecilian because he had forbidden a rich widow to bring to church an unauthorized bone of a martyr and kiss it before partaking of the Lord's Supper. Even more it seemed to them offensive that the decision should rest with the clergy as to who should be given the title of martyr. The situation in which the Donatists found themselves—under condemnation by the Church and the empire—restored to martyrdom its central position and entitled them to be considered the Church of the martyrs.

Nor were they disquieted because they were gaining the honored name of martyr more by strife than by suffering. Constantine told them precisely that deserved punishment is not martyrdom. The first instance in which martyrs turned into revolutionaries occurred only under a Christian emperor. The Donatists first appealed to the emperor, then took the sword. They had been discredited by the disclosure of apostasy on the part of some of their own bishops, and their conduct had done not a little to invalidate their claim. Nevertheless, they did not cease to cry, "What has the emperor to do with the Church?"

The answer was given in an angry letter of the emperor to Celsus, the vicar of Africa.[8] The emperor

8. *Urkunden*, p. 23.

learned from Celsus' report that he had at first suppressed the disturbance. Let him be indulgent. But
this he cannot be, for the Donatists, "who have separated themselves from the truth of God," are capable
of further crimes. The vicar should therefore an-
nounce to both parties the speedy coming of the emperor, who would declare to all the people and to the
clergy the proper way in which to honor the Godhead.
Those who did not comply he would "destroy and
annihilate."[9] He would himself incur great blame
were he not, in accord with his duty as a prince, to
drive out error and induce all with one voice to bring
true worship to the Almighty God.[10]

This document discloses pointedly the position Constantine was about to abandon. His assumption that
his reasoning was self-evident shows that it was a part
of the traditional concept of the imperial idea. That
his threat stood in conflict with the Edict of Milan and
with his entire religious policy[11] is no reason for

9. . . . . easdem personas, quae res istius modi concitant
faciuntque, ut non cum ea, quae oportet, veneratione summus
deus colatur, perdam atque discutiam (*Vita Constantini*, ed.
Heikel, p. 35, line 25).

10. Frend, p. 158, finds the same ideas in Constantine's
communication to the Synod of Tyre (*Vita Constantini*, ed.
Heikel, p. 4, line 42). But the threat there expressed says only
that if in the future a bishop should refuse to appear before
the synod, the emperor would send an official to teach him
that it is not seemly to resist measures taken by a ruler in the
interests of truth. The duty which, in the letter to Celsus,
Constantine assumed for himself is here ascribed to the verdict
of the bishops.

11. The authority to discover the good pleasure of God was

doubting its genuineness. The passionate tone serves as the emperor's own signature. One must expect new ideas to take time to expel contrary notions from the minds of their adherents. The juxtaposition of irreconcilables rather than the cold logic of the doctrinaire is the mark of a period of transition.

Much more significant is it that the principle announced by Constantine as universally applicable was actually applied only in the Christian area, in that very Church which had set itself against the Roman principle of constraint in religion and whose position Constantine had endorsed. Such an astonishing *volte face* is to be explained chiefly by the recourse of the defeated party to social disorders the government was bound to suppress. But even more important was the character of Constantine's calling, for he believed himself to have received a mission no less religious than political. The religious unity of mankind was not for Constantine, as for Diocletian, a heritage which however threatened should be at all costs maintained or restored; it was rather the highest of all goals. Since it

---

later ascribed by the emperor no longer merely to himself but to the great synod he assembled at Nicaea. He assured the congregations that the unity of the faith for which he strove— the pure love and simple piety—could not be brought into proper order unless all or at least most of the bishops came together and undertook an examination of that which is seemly in the service of God. Now he could say that everything had been scrupulously examined until the faith pleasing to God had come to light and could remain in doubt no longer (*Vita Constantini* 3.17; ed. Heikel, p. 84, lines 23 ff., 31 f.).

was to be achieved only on a Christian basis, the Church's assistance was indispensable.

To make the Church equal to the task was part of the emperor's mission. Her recruiting power should not be emasculated by schism. He had no thought of subjecting the Church to alien law when he fostered her inner and outer unity and as at Arles and Nicaea made possible its restoration. One may well assume that the close link that Constantine saw between his mission and that of the Church was what gave him the inner right to speak with such decisiveness and to lay down rules for the true worship of God to both groups, bishops and laity alike.

Thus far, Constantine had voiced simply the traditional view of the religious responsibility of the ruler. At the same time he took over significantly the correlative view that noncompliance was due to obstinacy.[12] Just as the pagan emperors held that their religious claims were resisted not by inner right but only by stubbornness, so Constantine was persuaded that those who refused to comply with his decision were actuated by "obstinacy" without any genuine grounds. He had investigated all their assertions and found them untenable. But unlike his predecessors he combined with obstinacy the concept of error, a guilty defection from the *veritas Dei*. The great controversy in which Constantine stood together with his generation and in which he sought to guide the decision was one that

12. *Urkunden*, No. 23, line 32, p. 35; No. 21, lines 8–12, p. 34.

extended into the conflict within the Church. His judgment with regard to the Donatists was now fixed. Their teaching and their behavior were instigated by the enemy of God, the devil. At this point there could be no further doubt or excuse.

Two qualifications may be recognized, though their extent cannot be definitely determined. One may wonder how much the sharpness of Constantine's word and the height of his pretensions rose from the anger in which the letter was written. Certainly later he did not claim so much. At Nicaea he was only a co-worker. Not through him and his rulership but through "the more than 300 bishops distinguished for life and learning" had God made known His will. The emperor referred to their word even though it was he who undertook to uphold this "bulwark of the faith."

The second qualification is that the diminution of the disorder enabled him to relax his countermeasures despite his principles, which went beyond the maintenance of the civil order. He was sure, however, that Donatism would flair up again, and therefore he had to go to the root of the evil. Indeed, before long new outbreaks of popular violence put an end to the provisional and conditional restraint. Then began the period of reprisals by the state. Lacking proof, we must assume that the principles of Constantine's letter were put into effect even though the promised visit of the emperor and the instruction to both parties did not take place. Though at the outset the wish of the Donatists to share in the emperor's favors may have brought him into the conflict, now more had come to be involved, namely the confiscation of churches and the banishment of bishops. Beyond this Constantine would not go, and no doubt military intervention and bloodshed occurred only when there was resistance. Equally sure is it that force did not break but rather increased the resistance of the Donatists. They boasted that they were martyrs and were all the more sure that they were right.

When it became apparent that the intervention of the state was of no avail, Constantine gave it up. Again we do not have the law that directed the officials to cease, but we do have a letter in which Constantine explained his reason to the Catholics of Africa and exhorted them to like behavior.[1]

If the emperor was now willing to substitute tolerance for the previous severity, he was a very long way from conceding that the Donatists were right. He justified his behavior and emphasized how restrained and Christian he had been. "What faith demanded, what prudence could do, what good intentions could contribute, all of this, as you know, I have attempted, and I have left nothing undone that humanity and moderation prescribe. This is the way, in accord with the dictates of our law, that the peace of the holy brotherhood is to be preserved." But no matter how good the emperor's intentions, they had not succeeded in taming "the power of their criminal intent instilled by the devil," under whose protection [2] the few false leaders

1. Ibid., No. 31.

had not abandoned their endeavors. In view of this obstinate resistance and of the numbers involved, nothing remained but to appeal to the help of almighty God, and in the meantime to be patient. The Catholic Christians should not retaliate but leave vengeance to God, who would count what they suffered as martyrdom. Soon, when the control of the ringleader slackened, men would come to see that they should not suffer themselves to be led by the few to eternal damnation, but rather that insight and repentance should lead them to eternal life.

Like Galerius on a previous occasion, Constantine here admitted a mistake but did not confess to fault. But unlike the heathen emperor, he did not propose a second best that would secure for the empire some heavenly protection. He did not see in the plurality of confessions an expression of inner riches, as if each had something of his own to contribute to the spiritual cosmos. The Donatists were inspired and hardened by nothing other than the breath of Satan. And against this only a heavenly remedy could avail. There was nothing left for men other than expectant submission, befitting "the people of the quiet law." [3] This demeanor, Constantine assumed, might have an influence on the crowds of Donatists, and their confidence might be shattered if they saw the demonic power of their leaders disappear before a higher power. They might

2. . . . favente adhuc sibi huic nequitiae patrocinio (ibid., No. 31, line 9, p. 51).

3. . . . quietae legis populus (line 24).

then turn and abandon their error. The emperor would not cease to hope for this in the case of the masses, even though he had abandoned hope for the leaders.

Constantine's goal was "the peace of the holy brotherhood." [4] Both the ineffective severity and the enforced tolerance seemed to him in conformity with the Christian law, the first because the intention was good and the means restrained and humane, the second because it committed punishment and healing to God and did not encroach upon His domain, for the well-meant human measures had proved unavailing.

*Indulgentia ignominiosissima* "most ignominious indulgence." [5] This is what Augustine called the tolerance of the Donatists by Constantine. The emperor dismissed their bishops though not without the sharpest reproof. He committed them to the judgment of the Lord which had already begun to work. Whereas the heathen were accorded an indulgence aimed at their reclamation, the heretics received a tolerance pointing to their shame. In both cases there was the admission that the imperial measures were not adequate in establishing the desired unity. But whereas the emperor granted to the adherents of the old cult time in which to be persuaded of a better course, in this instance the time was an interval in which the divine vengeance should operate without premature action on the part of man. In the first case, the Christians by their testimony were to help the heathen toward the true knowl-

4. . . . pax sanctissimae fraternitatis (line 5).
5. Ibid., No. 30.

98

edge, but here nothing remained to the Catholics save the exercise of tolerance and the endurance of suffering which would be accounted to them for martyrdom and would hasten the divine vengeance on their arrogant opponents. Here, too, the goal is not failure but conversion of others. The prospect in the case of the leaders of the sectaries was at any rate but slight. The exhortation to demonstrate the genuineness of faith through the exercise of patience was intended more for the consolation of those to whom it was addressed than for those whom one sought to win but who resisted all overtures.

But whatever the word, and whatever the mood, tolerance was proclaimed. All restrictions were removed, except that favors from the state were withheld. The policy which the emperor a few years before had said that he could not relinquish without grave guilt was now abandoned. It is significant that he no longer made a point of conscience out of that which formerly his imperial office did not allow. His persuasion of the necessity of the uniform worship of God was not shattered, and his judgment that the error of the Donatists imperiled the souls of the people had only been sharpened. How could he then allow their spokesmen to return, and how could he permit the sectaries to hold their religious assemblies?

In the case of weak emperors, the discrepancy between words and deeds is explained by the acuteness of their dilemma. And Constantine could not fail to see the need to end a policy which instead of succeeding had only made the situation worse. The recognition that imperial intervention had failed and the fear that severity might drive the obstinacy of the Donatists to open rebellion both pointed to a turn of the rudder. But that which is desirable and expedient is not automatically permissible. Constantine had never renounced his mission and had never sacrificed his higher goal to the wishes of the day. His sense of the realities was in conformity with his faith, and from it derived its power. His endeavor possessed its characteristic unity and its historical power only when the political appeared also as a religious possibility or necessity, when that which the state demanded could be construed as the command of God. When he was using the arm of the state against the godless movement, faith and expediency were united in regarding the banishment of the leaders and the confiscation of their places of assembly as sufficient. But now the recognition of failure—"the obstinacy proved to be untameable"—compelled him to face the question. In view of their resistance he became aware of the limit to the power of the state, or rather he found it more narrow than he had supposed: even earlier he had recognized limits, since moderation and humanity were demanded by the very faith he was seeking to uphold. This insight was earlier and clearer than the lesson of political expediency.

The realization that superhuman powers were involved and that these powers both impelled and protected the heretics led the emperor to look for divine help, which alone could effect anything under these circumstances. This was in accord with Constantine's experience, because he had sought divine assistance against demonic powers. He was mindful also of the divine admonition: "'vengeance is mine,' saith the Lord" (Romans 12:19). This means that Constantine's view of providence and faith in history reckoned on the perceptible intervention of God and the victory of the good, and in all this on the operation of a higher power. He recognized at the same time the conditions under which alone it could be expected, namely a patient endurance of suffering without retaliation and an unshaken adherence to the Christian way.

Thus a religious basis was found for the *indulgentia ignominiosissima*.[6] This meant nothing other than a relinquishment of human punishment, because the offender who hitherto had relied on the supernatural power which inspired and upheld him is now given over to the wrath of God. Constantine looked for a subjugation of every demonic power, which could not stand against the power of God. When the adherents of the Donatist leaders became aware of their weakness, they would no longer allow themselves to be misled. In this way one might hope that the masses of the Donatists would come to their senses. Through

6. The Emperor Julian, according to Ammianus Marcellinus (22.5.3 f.), exercised another sort of *indulgentia ignominiosissima*—to be sure, only as an afterthought—when he recalled the Nicene bishops banned under Constantius. For Julian's policy of tolerance see Joseph Bidez, *La Vie de l'Empereur Julien* (1930), *3, 5.*

such a detour this form of tolerance also might exercise a power of persuasion by obedience to the biblical command to let God have full sway, and demonstrate His superiority to the demonic powers. Then the Donatist rank and file might be brought from their utter unreasonableness to a sound mind.

That these ideas with which Constantine justified the dishonorable tolerance of the Donatists were not simply of the moment was made plain a decade later. In the Numidian town of Cirta, later (and to this day) called Constantine, the Donatists had their headquarters. Here the fanatical horde had taken over a church built by the emperor and had refused to give it up. The Catholics accepted the situation and requested another place in which to build another church. The answer of the emperor [7] brings again to light the principles at which he had arrived in the course of this controversy. Here his judgment of the heretics received its sharpest and most clear-cut expression, integrating the whole of Constantine's religious and political thought.

The will of the creator has an eye to the unity of humanity. It is clear that whatever is divisive is devised by the enemy of God. What the heretics undertake is done at his instigation. He possesses their minds and their thoughts. How then can anyone who, through error freely chosen, apostatizes from God to the devil do anything other than that which is contrary to

7. *Urkunden,* No. 36.

equity and justice? No wonder then if the unrighteous separate themselves from the good!

On the other hand the command of faith demands abstention from all strife. For that reason the emperor highly approved of the patience exhibited by the Catholics in Cirta. They had done wisely and well to yield and not to provoke the enemy to open rebellion. These people, like their head, should be overcome by patience, which brings to those who exercise it a greater glory but to those who refuse to forsake their unrighteousness a greater judgment. God calls himself the avenger and therefore all vengeance must be left to Him. But the emperor would not cease to remind and to exhort. Perhaps the truths granted to the offenders might bring some to their right mind. If they would obey his council they would be free from all blame. Admittedly the hope now was slight. "They want to die in their evil." [8] "We wish to guard our own and follow our way." [9] The emperor's procedure corresponded to these principles. The church he had himself built he left to the Donatists, and built for the Catholics a new one.

In general the stand taken by Constantine was justified even though his hopes for its persuasive power

8. Constat eos in sua malitia manere et in suis facinoribus mori velle (ibid., line 87, p. 56).

9. Nos tamen, fratres, sequamur quae nostra sunt, mandatis instemus, custodiamus divina praecepta, ex bonis actibus vitam nostram ab erroribus vindicantes favente dei misericordia per rectum limitem dirigamus (ibid., line 90, p. 56).

proved illusory. The government could afford to take no action against the Donatists, since expansion beyond the boundaries of their initial territory was short-lived or inconsequential. They had no thought of separating Africa from the empire or of setting up a counter-emperor. There was no point then in using the army against them and of setting citizen against citizen, for which Constantine reproached his predecessors. The success of the Donatists whether repressed or liberated was, to be sure, considerable. Toward the end of Constantine's reign they assembled in Carthage a synod of 270 bishops,[1] although some of them represented only very small localities. Nevertheless the number justified the judgment of St. Jerome when he said that "Donatus had misled nearly the whole of Africa."

No less important than the political results was the fundamental decision imposed upon the emperor by his experiences with the Donatists and the failure of his forceable measures. It was concerned with a religious justification. One should not detract from its significance by treating it as merely rationalization, a face-saving device to conceal a political defeat. Constantine confessed without any concealment that his attempt had not succeeded and that he had come to the end of his resources. But if one takes the religious grounds at face value, they help us to understand the peculiar quality of this tolerance—namely to leave the guilt to a higher tribunal than that of men, with hope for the masses of those misled. At the same time, plac-

1. Ibid., No. 38.

ing heresy in the context of a great metaphysical conflict paved the way for the legislation against the heretics of the later emperors. Devoid as they were of the human moderation and the Christian restraint of Constantine, they found in his view of heresy as guilty error, as the denial of God and a return to the devil, the warrant not for tolerance, not even for a dishonorable tolerance, but only for the most severe intolerance.

In the meantime, Constantine did have one more hope of healing the breach, as soon as "the enemy of the world" [2] was overcome. He would send bishops from the East, and especially from Egypt, to Africa that as "leaders of the salvation of the people" [3] they might restore unanimity to the factions. He described this as his most pressing concern.[4]

All the greater was his distress when he discovered that here too a schism had broken out, which rendered the Eastern Church unfit for the work of unification. Thereupon the emperor sent a detailed letter [5] to both parties in the theological controversy: Alexander, the bishop of Alexandria, and Arius, the Presbyter, who gave his name to the great dispute. The emperor significantly offered himself to both as a mediator. Even if the matter were of great importance, peace, he

2. "The enemy of the world" in this instance has reference not to Licinius but to the demonic power standing behind him. Cf. *Selbstzeugnis*, p. 56, n. 1.

3. *Vita Constantini* 2.66–67.

4. Ibid., 2.65.67.

5. Ibid., 2.64–72; ed. Heikel, pp. 67–71.

thought, should not be difficult to achieve. "You, Alexander asked the presbyters what each of them thought about a certain passage in the law, yes, and what each thought about an inconsequential part of a question, and you, Arius, have rashly proposed what should have never been thought of or should have been passed over in silence. Thereby the fellowship of the churches is denied and the people split in twain." [6] If, then, the Church is rent by a mere contention over words, the imperial arbitrator could with even greater propriety demand respectful attention to his counsel. Since the essentials of the law were not involved in the dispute, since no new worship of God was being introduced, since the kernel of the faith was not affected, strife and schism were intolerable: "I do not compel you to be of one mind over this very simple question." [7] Peace and fellowship can be maintained even though there may be differences of opinion with regard to trivial matters: "We do not all like the same things and each does not have the same nature and way of thinking as another." [8] Of course with regard to God and his work in the world there must be one faith, one understanding, and full agreement. But if you do not agree in minor matters, let each be of his own mind. "Unity among one another," "belief

6. Ibid., c. 69; p. 68, line 19.
7. Ibid., c. 71; p. 70, line 20.
8. Line 24: μηδὲ πάντες ἐν ἅπασι ταὐτὸν βουλόμεθα, μηδὲ μία τις ἐν ἡμῖν φύσις ἢ γνώμη πολιτεύεται.

106

in the truth," "honor to God and to the service of the law"—these must remain in full force.[9]

Here the judgment of the emperor was made unmistakably plain as to the rank of the controversy: nothing more than a squabble over words divided the Church. But if Constantine had no feeling for the great issues involved, he voiced a maxim which subsequently met with wide endorsement—that if agreement could not be reached, one should be silent with regard to the point at issue. The Church should take a lesson from the philosophers who agree in fundamentals and without acrimony debate minor points. The peace of the Church comes first, perhaps not absolutely every time but ordinarily, and for the time being the emperor did not see that this controversy dealt with one of the few questions that demand universal consideration.

In the theological dispute of the Eastern Church, Constantine spoke a word of tolerance. Though he was quickly to find out that this dispute was no more to be reconciled than that in Africa, his attempt at any rate is significant, and the way that he proposed repeatedly commended itself later as a device for refuting error and reconciling bitter contention. Constantine's attitude was not that of a neutral and indifferent statesman who did not wish to see the civil peace and political

9. Line 30: τὸ μέντοι τῆς κοινῆς φιλίας ἐξαίρετον καὶ ἡ τῆς ἀληθείας πίστις ἥ τε περὶ τὸν θεὸν καὶ τὴν τοῦ νόμου θρησκείαν τιμὴ μενέτω παρ' ὑμῖν ἀσάλευτος.

order disturbed by questions of the faith and would therefore tolerate everything. He was far from divorcing the fate of the empire from the religion of its inhabitants. The true worship of God was the very question for the life of the empire, and the decisive question for him and for his time was the religious one. But if in crucial matters there could be no hesitation and no deviation if divine grace were not to be withdrawn from the empire, he nevertheless distinguished the essential from the nonessential that could be left free for everyone to affirm and hold his own opinion. Of course the limit of his understanding is apparent when he could treat as a mere bout of words the problem of the relationship of Christ to God; and he himself did not continue to adhere to this opinion. But the differentiation between the essential and the nonessential was to have a long and agitated history, in which, to be sure, the line between that which is binding upon all and that which can be left to individual discretion has been drawn very differently in different times and has itself revealed the quality of the teaching. There is no unanimity as to where the true middle lies. For Constantine the fundamentals were the uniform worship of God, the unbroken fellowship and "faith in the truth." On these points there must be agreement. If this be assured, freedom may be allowed for the remainder. If each is prepared to concede to the other, nothing is needed other than an appeal to good will to restore the broken peace. This means, of course, readiness to drop the points at issue, or at any rate not to parade them before the people. The dangerous and yet so appealing advice to leave thorny questions to the theologians or to avoid them altogether found in Constantine's letter an ingenuous expression. The popular counsel to subordinate dogmatic to ethical questions and to place love above faith is proclaimed in this anxious letter of the emperor.

Constantine, speedily recognizing that the way he proposed was unacceptable, repeated the attempts he had made in the West, only on a larger scale. He summoned a council, to which he invited not only the bishops of the East but also representatives from the West, so that this should be what it has always since been called, the first ecumenical council. At this gathering at Nicaea, the Church itself, in collaboration with the emperor, was to answer the disquieting questions, or rather give expression to God's answer. Now it was no longer a matter of trivial differences but, as the emperor himself had come to see, of the cleavage dividing truth from error. But error had no right in the Church and no right in the state. Whereas earlier both parties had assumed and pretended too much, now the one servant of the devil responsible for disturbing the peace of the Church by the dissemination of error was Arius. The assembly at Nicaea, through the pronouncement "of the more than 300 bishops distinguished by life and learning," had once and for all established a norm by which in future the true teaching could be measured and assured.[1]

Nevertheless, the principles of Constantine's peace letter were not entirely given up. The point was not only that he was unhappy over the separation of the Arian group from the Catholic Church, but that he did everything possible to extend the peace achieved at Nicaea. This dangerous course was to lead —partly during the lifetime of Constantine and more particularly afterward—into a whirlpool. But if the teaching of Arius could no longer be relegated to the area of private opinion to which it had been consigned by the emperor's first letter, even that letter affirmed the principle that there are some fundamentals from which no deviation can be allowed. Nicaea had simply placed the error of Arius in this other category as imperiling the Christian faith. Constantine accepted this norm. Anyone who resisted the decision of Nicaea would incur the imperial displeasure and be sent into banishment, because he injured the unity of the Church. On the other hand, the emperor hoped by this measure to change the mind of Arius, so that he could be received back into the Christian Church.

For our question, of special importance is the close connection in both time and content between the Council of Nicaea and the Edict against Heretics, which served as the basis for all subsequent legislation on heresy by the Christian emperors.

1. Constantine to the Catholic Church of Alexandria: Athanasius, 3.1.25; "Werke," ed. Opitz (above, p. 30, n. 3), p. 53.

The most important document for Constantine's attitude to the heretics is this Edict,[2] which shortly after Nicaea imposed the decision there reached upon the Christian sect which rejected it.

"Be it known to you Novatianists, Valentinians, Marcionites, Paulicians and those called Phrygians, together with all heretics in general, with what lies your folly has been ensnared." The document goes on to upbraid the enemies of the truth, the opponents of the life, those who seduce to destruction. Not only do they themselves fall into disaster, but with highest pretense they deceive others: confuse blameless consciences and deny to the faithful the light. The enraged lawgiver has not the time to catalog all the nonsense they amass, and he will refrain from further details lest he harm someone by the mere recital. Instead of portraying the damage, it is better promptly to heal it. "The long delay has been the reason why some of the healthy have been infected by this plague. Why not then strike at the root of so great an evil by the public proclamation of my disfavor?" Since the corruption can no longer be endured, the emperor forbids any assemblies of heretics, assigns their "so-called

2. *Vita Constantini* 3.64–65; ed. Heikel, p. 111. Cf. *Selbstzeugnis*, pp. 82 ff. The "law" and the "teaching" mentioned by Eusebius (*Vita Constantini* 3.63; p. 111, line 10): πρὸς δὲ τῷ νόμῳ καὶ ζωοποιὸν διδασκαλίαν εἰς αὐτῶν πρόσωπον διετύπου refer not to two documents of which one has been lost, but to the "teaching" section incorporated in the Edict (*Vita Constantini* 3.64–65) describes itself as "law" (65, p. 112, line 10: διὰ τοῦ νόμου τούτου). It is addressed to those with whose assemblies and properties it has to do.

houses of prayer" to the Church, and confiscates their other property. He who desires true religion may enter the Catholic Church and thus come to the knowledge of truth. Errors must no longer imperil the good fortune of our time. It befits the blessings which God has conferred upon us that all those who hope for future blessing should be brought back to the true way, from darkness to light, from folly to truth, from death to redemption. The public and private sources of infection are therefore to be destroyed.

Constantine conceived it to be his duty from then on to lead men into the right way. He was responsible not only for the outward but also for the inward, the eternal salvation of his subjects. The same experience which led to tolerance of the heathen, namely the good fortune which had been his lot, drove him now to deny it to the heretics. Since the previous indulgence instead of curing the sick had infected the well, the severe course on which he was now embarked was regarded as medicine for the benefit of the heretics themselves and also of those who otherwise would be infected by them. "For this work of healing I have instituted the necessary force."

Eusebius discerningly brings this law into relation with the decision of the Council of Nicaea. "As the emperor overcame the divisions and brought the Church of God to unanimous harmony, he thought to remove another sort of godless men as dangerous to the life of mankind." [3] The chronological nearness is apparent from the date of the Edict relative to the

3. *Vita Constantini* 3.63; p. 110, line 30.

Novatianists on September 25, 326,[4] which exempted this group from the general regulations against the heretics because they were dogmatically orthodox and merely schismatic. The inner connection lies in the efforts of Constantine for unity. After the success of the Council against the Arians, he would extend his plan to overcome all the other divisions. The truth discovered at Nicaea, God's own directive, is binding upon all Christians. But since the essence of the Church for Constantine consisted not only in the dogmatic propositions but no less in ethical demands, among which the obligation to unity was pre-eminent, Nicaea was held to provide the norm to which all Christians must conform, including those who had seceded earlier.

Eusebius, who records this remarkable document, uses in his introduction [5] some of the expressions and thoughts of the Edict: "By pious pretense they endangered the cities." The public life of the state appeared to him also to be imperiled by the Christian schismatics. Therefore the officials to whom the Edict was addressed were obligated "to root out the ill-famed clan," even though the lawgiver addressed himself directly to the schismatics, presenting to them "the life-giving teaching" and summoning them to repentance. At one point we observe a certain discrepancy between the account of Eusebius and the text of the Edict, because the text does not speak of banishment, whereas Eusebius talks about "driving

4. Cf. *Selbstzeugnis,* pp. 193 f.
5. *Vita Constantini* 3.63.

out." Now it could be that the officials, enforcing the Edict against indomitable opposition, had recourse to expulsions; this would very well fit the expression used by Eusebius.[6] But however that may be, the Edict says nothing about it. One is tempted to assume that Constantine was affected by his experiences in the banishment of the Donatist bishops. At any rate, as previously, nothing is said about imprisonment and fines. The sharp denunciations of the first part of the Edict go far beyond the deeds mentioned in the second part. And if one thinks of threats issued against the Arians, one may see once again truly operative in this Edict against the heretics that humanity and moderation of which Constantine spoke when he looked back on his dealings with the Donatists.

The postscript of Eusebius expressed great satisfaction: by this Edict the lurking places of the unorthodox were dispersed, and the "wild beasts," the leaders of their godliness, were driven out.[7] Constantine thus had no doubt about his authority, even though the experience with the Donatists had disclosed the limits to all action on the part of the state. After Nicaea he tried with the eastern schismatics the very same methods that had proved untenable in Africa. He

6. Ibid.; ed. Heikel, page 111, line 10, where the ἐλαύνειν, to be sure, does not refer directly to the law or to the officials but to the emperor himself: καταπεμφὲν δέ τι τοῖς κατ᾿ ἔθνος ἡγεμόσι ⟨πρόσταγμα⟩ πᾶν τὸ τῶν τοιούτων δύσφημον φῦλον ἤλαυνεν. And 3.66, p. 113, line 5: ἠλαύνοντό τε οἱ θῆρες οἱ [τε] τῆς τούτων δυσσεβείας ἔξαρχοι.

7. Ibid. 3; p. 113, line 4.

forbade assemblies, assigned the churches to the Catholics, and may have begun to ban the leaders of the opposition. Eusebius celebrated this action against rival groups as one of the glories of his emperor. To be sure, his own words show that the Church did not expect uniform success among these who were thus to be reclaimed. They were not to be received back without examination. The officials of the Church, said Eusebius,[8] must make a careful investigation and must keep all the hypocrites from the fold as wolves in sheep's clothing. Others might be accepted after a probationary period. The Church assumed the right of sifting and treated the schismatics differently from the heretics. The triumphant conclusion mentioned no further reservation. "Thus shone alone the Catholic

8. At any rate, Eusebius shows indirectly that a problem is created for the Church by the emperor's directive to the religiously interested heretics to attach themselves to the Church. For Augustine, entry into the Church at the behest of the state constituted a very serious question, which troubled him no little until he arrived, as he thought, at a solution. He justified the constraint, but only with hesitation could he condone the punishment. In no case would Constantine compel *all* heretics to come in but only those "concerned for the true and pure word of God." He would not induce an undifferentiated mass movement into the Church but would impel only the better sort. The question whether some might not be converted for reasons of expediency did not yet engage him. But the leaders of the Church could not leave this question without an answer. Eusebius is an unimpeachable witness that at this point the judgment of the Church and the state were at variance. This is one of the few places where he took a view other than that of his hero.

Church of God, since nowhere on earth was there a heretical or schismatic group remaining."

Among the list of the heretics enumerated we miss not only the Donatists but also the parallel "church of the martyrs" that arose during the time of the persecution in Egypt—namely the Meletians. They received at Nicaea the same sort of treatment as that accorded to the Donatists at Arles and at Rome. They were treated as schismatics whose bishops, if they merely came over to the main body of the Church, would be received in all honor. These Meletians also were not content with the judgment rendered and gave Athanasius no end of trouble, granted that they in their turn had reason to complain of many severities. Constantine was unquestionably in accord with the mediatory policy of the council. He among the Meletians who made his peace with the Catholic Church was assured of imperial commendation. To the emperor's mind only contentiousness and pettiness stood in the way of doing "that which is pleasing to God"— namely returning to the fellowship of the Church.[9] By the same token his wrath fell upon "those accursed, perverted, godless Meletians hardened in their infatuation,"[1] since their accusations against the bishop of Alexandria appeared to him entirely unsubstantiated. Yet he listened to their complaints, which in the end

9. Constantine to John Archaph—Athanasius, *Apologia Secunda;* "Werke," ed. Opitz, p. 148, line 15: μικροψυχία; line 18: ἀψιμαχία.

1. Ibid., p. 113, line 24.

contributed to undermining the position of Athanasius at the court. All in all, the emperor's treatment of the Meletians simply confirms what we have observed elsewhere in his attitude to the heretics: the wish to bring them back to the communion of the Church did not blunt the sharpness of his judgment on their reprehensible separation regardless of their teaching, because the command of unanimity belonged to the most fundamental of the teachings.

Not only the Meletians gained the ear of the emperor for their complaints, but also the Novatianists, with their petitions.[2] Unlike the other heretics they might retain their houses and cemeteries. This proviso meant undoubtedly that they might use their houses— that is to say, enjoy the right of assembly. Thereby the Edict against the Heretics was in their case canceled. Only the property from the time before the separation remained with the churches of "perpetual holiness." The Catholic Church alone is the heir of the early Church. Since the Novatianists accepted the Nicene doctrine, the emperor must have interpreted "holiness" in broader terms than those of dogmatic rectitude. At the point of orthodoxy they were among the holy, but their schism deprived them of one of the essential marks of the Christian religion: to be of one mind. It is instructive to observe that here Constantine followed the viewpoint of his ecclesiastical advisers, for whom the

2. *Cod. Theod.* 16.5.2 (326, Sept. 25). Cf. *Selbstzeugnis*, p. 193.

orthodoxy and the severe moral discipline of the Novatianists removed them from the class of the heretics who had no claim to any favor.

A letter of Constantine to the congregation at Alexandria,[3] where the Arian controversy had had its rise, communicated the decisions of Nicaea and contrasted Arius, that "infamous son of a devil," with the "more than 300 bishops distinguished in life and learning" who had done their utmost to establish one and the same faith. "Only Arius showed himself addicted to the devil, so that he sowed this godlessness first among you and then among others." Thus "being convicted of error he is deprived of honor." Objection to the condemnation not only of the teaching but also of the life of the heresiarch led to the banishment of two of his advocates—the bishops Eusebius of Nikomedia and Theognis of Nicaea.[4] They accomplished their reinstatement only by recognizing the "PEACE"—that is, by abandoning Arius. The emperor, who always held to the dogmatic and ecclesiastical decisions of his council, sought even to win the dissident Arians. This did not mean any alteration of principle. His point was rather to reclaim Arius for the faith declared

3. Athanasius, 3.1.25; ed. Opitz, p. 53. Cf. *Selbstzeugnis*, p. 68.

4. The banishment of Eusebius of Nikomedia and Theognis was explained by the emperor not so much as an act of state as the execution of a divine judgment: "Divine providence has expelled them from their people, for it could not allow innocent souls to be corrupted by the insanity of the few" (Athanasius, 3.1.28).

at Nicaea. A written communication from Arius [5] avoiding all the propositions condemned by the council seemed sufficient to satisfy the requirement. Arius was thereupon invited to the court and in conversation gave the impression that he was in agreement with the authoritative creed. Constantine turned to Bishop Alexander with the demand that he satisfy himself as to Arius' change of mind and if persuaded of its genuineness that he readmit him to the Church.[6] With greater emphasis the same demand was laid upon the young successor of the aged bishop, Athanasius. "In recognition of my will you shall give unimpeded entry to all those who wish to enter the churches." [7] The bishop was actually threatened with deposition and banishment if he refused to comply. Nevertheless, Constantine accepted the determined reply of the inflexible Athanasius that he had discovered no change in the teaching of those condemned. Several years went by, in which, indeed the whole of Constantine's purpose was not accomplished, but it so altered the way to be taken that realization of the plan appeared feasible. In the interim he had once more repudiated the accused, this time with a sharp rejection of his person and his teaching—and this in a law whose essentials, if not its wording, are conserved for us in the

5. Arius to Constantine, Athanasius, 3.1.30. Cf. *Selbstzeugnis*, p. 78.
6. Athanasius, 3.1.32. *Selbstzeugnis*, p. 80.
7. Athanasius, *Apologia secunda*, 59.6; ed. Opitz, p. 2, line 140.

*Codex* of Theodosius II. This emperor expressly appealed to Constantine's regulation.[8] "The harsh letter" to Arius [9] which took up his teaching in detail extended also at the end to his followers, to whose numbers Arius appears to have called attention, thus greatly irritating the monarch, who now decreed that they should be saddled with exceptional taxes. "The rain of power" would extinguish the glaring flames of Arius; his followers would learn to sweat under the imposts if they did not quickly come over to the inviolable faith.

Even more severe was the Arian Edict of 333. Arius, who imitated the wicked and godless, must be subject to the same dishonor. Just as the name of Porphyry, who composed the godless writings against the Christians, had been disgraced and his writings destroyed, even so should Arius and his followers be called Porphyrians and their writings should be

8. Athanasius, 3.1.33. *Selbstzeugnis*, p. 103.

9. Athanasius, 3.1.34. *Selbstzeugnis*, p. 112. The attempt of H. Kraft, p. 233, to eliminate from the "hot" letter its theological polemical portion, by far the larger part, and to ascribe it to Athanasius breaks down, partly because of the uniform quality, which admits of no division, and also because of the characterization of the letter by Epiphanius: "Burning with zeal, the emperor sent a great encyclical to the entire Roman empire against Arius and his faith, a letter full of wisdom and true words" (*Panarion* 69.9.3; *GCS*, ed. Holl, p. 159, line 25). "Zeal" precisely fits the "great" letter and the expressions "wisdom and true words" would exactly describe from the point of view of Epiphanius a theological refutation of the heresiarch through the monarch who on occasion celebrated also spiritual victories.

burned, that no memory of them survive. Secret pos-
session of the books would incur death.

This *damnatio memoriae* corresponds to the frequent usage of Constantine which the Church has been
all too ready to accept. The burning of the anti-
Christian books of Porphyry was a countermeasure to
Diocletian's destruction of Christian writings. As to
the execution of Constantine's law, we know nothing.
The extension of this threat to heretical writings as
well as the proclamation of the death penalty for resistance is to be attributed to the impulsive emperor
rather than to be regarded as an actual fulfillment of
the repressive law, which appears to have been in effect only briefly. Two years later there was a return
to the way of mediation. This time it was Athanasius
who appeared to Constantine to stand in the way of
reconciliation. To the Synod of Tyre, which condemned Athanasius and then proceeded to the dedication of the Church of the Holy Sepulchre at Jerusalem
(A.D. 335), again Constantine presented the question he
had formerly directed to Bishop Alexander—whether
the faith of Arius expressed in a written confession was
not in accord with sound Apostolic teaching.[1] The
Synod gave an affirmative answer[2] and thus made
possible the reinstatement of the one whom Nicaea
had condemned. Just before this solemn act of re-

1. Constantine to Alexander of Alexandria: Athanasius,
13.1.32. Cf. *Selbstzeugnis*, p. 80.
2. Synod of Jerusalem to Alexandria. Athanasius, *De syno-
dis* 21.2–7. Cf. *Selbstzeugnis*, p. 118.

habilitation, Arius died in Constantinople. Constantine's policy of unification was then taken up by his sons, with an obvious leaning to the faith condemned at Nicaea.

What is the reason for the remarkable discrepancy between Constantine's tolerance of the heathen and his intolerance of the heretics?

To the heathen Constantine granted the freedom of personal decision, although their cult was fraught with the power of corruption. But the heretics also were the enemies of God, guilty of falling away from Him, of turning from truth to error, and of disloyalty to their own law. These broke the fellowship to which they had once belonged.

In the case of the heathen, there was the hope that they would come to see what the hour demanded of them. "With the help of the providence of the redeemer God a great crowd of men had dedicated themselves to the Holy Church." [3] After the driving out of the dragon from the administration of the empire, the power of God was manifest to all. "Now those who had been restrained hitherto by fear, disbelief, and sin might come to knowledge." Constantine was the spokesman of a missionary, expanding Church and saw in heathenism the defeated power whose adherents, some earlier and some later, would voluntarily come to sanity and decision if given time.

On the other hand, the heretics were Christians

3. Constantine to Eusebius: *Vita Constantini* 4.36; ed. Heikel, p. 131, line 19. Cf. ibid. 3.17.

who also had been accorded the grace of the hour and yet were not reclaimed by patient waiting. The patience granted them had served rather to reduce their sanity. The schismatics increased rather than decreased. Hope at best could be entertained only for the misguided rank and file, not for the incorrigible leaders. The endangered masses had to be protected while the seducers were to be rooted out. Only when such measures prove fruitless and the fanaticism of the mob breaks out more violently must the ruler be restrained and hope that God will step in to curb and break the demonic forces which have instigated the leaders, that thus the people may be brought to their senses. The whole power of the state has an ally in the better knowledge on the part of the heretics, who cannot deny the command contained in their own law. The state demands only what God demands. Besides, since at Nicaea all the undecided questions received their answer and God Himself declared His will through the decision of so many worthy bishops, no Christian had any ground or right to doubt or stand aside. United faith and united worship were incumbent upon all. Although the heathen and the heretics thus formed a common front and obeyed the same diabolic power, they were not to be judged in the same way. The heretics knew what the heathen had yet to learn. No alien yoke was placed upon them if they were required to obey what they could not deny. To them was allowed or from them was demanded that which the Christian law itself does not permit in the case of the heathen.

To the Christian splinter groups Constantine refused what he had granted to the heathen. But the law concerning heretics must be seen in the context of its age. We must note not merely the limits it imposes on tolerance but also the fact that Constantine breaks through them on several occasions. Of course the exceptions do not eliminate the law, and the reasons given for them do not attain the depth of those proffered for the toleration of the heathen. However, the emperor's attitude toward the Christian heretics does not actually belong to the moment of history which we have considered. The issues and insights that determined the emperor's life and work are to be pin-pointed where religious and state concerns meet in his personal history. By comparison the small Christian groups are of peripheral significance. In this matter neither the demand on him nor his reply reveals a total engagement of his person. Even where he tried an uncharted path and sought for a solution of his own, as in the case of the Donatists, his measures seem left-handed in comparison to the edict concerning the heathen. This fact prevents the sort of straightforward contrast between the difference in treatment meted out to heretics and heathen that would put in question his toleration of the latter. But precisely because it stands on the periphery, the law about heretics assures an unimpeded view as well as a proper understanding of the height of Constantine's achievement in his hour of history.

In that hour, at the apex of his career, conscious of his victory and mission, the emperor was called upon to equal with his reply the greatness of the moment. By contrast the law concerning heretics clearly belongs among the exigencies of the daily round.

For this, if for no other, reason there is no need to confirm the edict concerning the heathen by means of an examination of Constantine's reign as a whole.[4] The moment and its task were the measure of the action appropriate to them. Encounter with an hour of history—and that is what we are here concerned with—is not the same as opening a vista upon an ecclesiastical or secular saint whose actions must always prove exemplary. Nor has our attention stayed with that which turned out to be historically effective. Theodosius continued the process begun with the law concerning heretics, whereas the edict concerning the heathen found no following.

4. Examples of later legislation would lead us to expect that if a differentiation is made between heathen and heretics, tolerance would be graded in accord with the amount of agreement. In that case the highest degree of indulgence would be accorded the orthodox Christian sectaries and the least to the heathen. Instead, we find Constantine's procedure to have been precisely the reverse.

One would have expected that if tolerance were graded, the highest would have been accorded to the orthodox Christian sectaries and the lowest to the heathen. The reverse was true for Constantine, as also for Aquinas, though not for the same reason. His principle was: Accipere fidem est voluntatis, sed tenere eam acceptam est necessitatis: *Summa Theologica* 11.2, *quaest.* 10–11.

# Conclusion

THE EXPECTATION of Constantine that some day all men would arrive by free consent at a unified faith has proved illusory, as it was bound to do. The subsequent emperors held fast to the goal and thought to achieve it through the arm of the state. They lost thereby the way of the first Christian emperor.

Today—what historical convulsions lie between!—all citizens of the state share in political responsibility and the rulers are subject to election and removal. Constantine, who adhered to one party, was able to tolerate the other in the hope that they would soon be persuaded of the truth of his position; but what for him was to be an interim solution now appears to us as continuous. The religiously neutral state corresponds to our concept of the political responsibility of all citizens for the regulation of the commonweal, however much private as well as public life appears to us to be the testing ground for our faith. We are prevented from imitating the first Christian emperor both by the insight, attested by long historical experience, that faith is not everybody's preference and by the fact that power no longer resides in the hands of a single ruler.

But the point of prime importance is that faith itself demands modesty with regard to the pretensions of a Christian empire. The purity of the word is at stake. When the state with its instruments comes to the help of the Gospel, it serves to undermine rather than to buttress.[1] The misunderstanding is all too easy that the word is a more refined form of the law, a part of the order of the state, validated to be sure not so much by earthly as by more potent heavenly rewards and punishments. To heed, in today's different situation, the call of Constantine's hour means to do more than simply renounce, as he did, the use of force; it further demands that we forswear, as he did not, all external assistance on behalf of faith. Therefore the state must refrain from intervention in an area where a boundary is set to force and where nothing else can work and win save the powerless word.

There is a second consideration to which this conclusion points, namely the ground for tolerance. Furthermore, a merely formal tolerance, based only on negotiations, is not secure against sudden reverse. We have an unshakable foundation only if we come to the realization that faith itself demands freedom, and in faith freedom possesses its best protection. May we then change the word of the ancient church, that it is not proper to religion to compel religion, to the positive statement: it is proper to faith to respect the faith of

1. Cf. Hilarius, *Contra Arianos vel Auxentium* (Migne, *PL*, 10.610); cf. also Luther to Spalatin, Nov. 4, 1520: Non est principum . . . tueri verbum Dei.

another as much as its own? Thus whoever endangers liberty threatens truth itself. The more lofty a value, the more exposed it is, and it is a sign of its exalted nature that freedom participates in the fate of truth—a fate of derision, denial, and combat. Both are suppressed together, and together they rise out of their humiliation. The proper atmosphere of faith makes men not slaves but free.

The gospel itself tells of the conflict between tolerance and intolerance. When the Samaritans refused hospitality to Jesus, because his face was set to go to Jerusalem, the disciples asked him whether they should bring down fire from heaven and consume them, as Elias had done. He answered (Luke 9:55), "Ye know not what spirit ye are of." This word restrained the disciples from vengeance upon those who would not receive their Lord. Here intolerance appeared in its most intelligible form. It is, or appears to be, simply a holy zeal which intervenes on behalf of faith and fidelity and is not self-seeking. The honor of a person or a cause is sacred before the eyes of those who believe in them, and an affront to these is a crime to be expiated. Not however by the hand of man—vengeance is left to God. Intolerance has not always been so restrained.

And yet, said Luther, even this is an evil zeal, not from God but from the devil.[2] The disciples had to be turned around. Here Jesus was going against the

2. Cf. Luther, sermon on Luke 9:51 ff. (1537); Weimar ed., t. 45, p. 407.

Church, said Luther, and it was on the question of tolerance that the Church was rebuked. The disciples were not pointed toward the example of Jesus himself, or toward the rights of men; nor were they exhorted to take a more sympathetic view of the Samaritans. Rather, the disciples were reminded of the power by which they lived and which alone could govern their lives, namely the Holy Spirit.[3]

Tolerance is here neither a law nor a right but a working of that which man can deny and to which he must be recalled, the fountain of faith and the lord of all good works. God Himself intervenes on behalf of men, even of those who reject Him. He chides the most warranted indignation and rejects every correction by force. He confers freedom in a form not to be grasped, comprehended, or systematized, yet operative in the course of history as the Spirit of Christ.

3. One may wonder whether Luther's statement, which was cited against him by the bull of excommunication, may not have been derived from this text. It said, "To burn heretics is against the will of the *Spirit*"—Hereticos comburi est contra voluntatem *spiritus*. Indeed, the "Assertio" of the phrase (Weimar ed., *t.* 7, pp. 139 f.) refers to Luke 9:54 ff.: "Hoc est, quod et ego disci et dico Christro magistro, eos, qui igne persequuntur homines non esse boni spiritus filios huius tunc? mali spiritus, qui erat homicidu ab initio. Christus non voluit vi et igne cagere homines ad fidem. Dedit ob id gladium spiritus, ut in hoc pugnareut, qui sui spiritus filii sunt" (p. 139, lines 31–38). ". . . nulli cogendi sunt ad fidem, sed spiritui sancto dandus est locus et honor, ut spiret ubi vult" (*t.* 12, p. 194). Cf. Roland A. Bainton, *Here I Stand* (1950), pp. 375–78.

"Ye know not what spirit ye are of." This reminder provides a surer basis for tolerance than any law or reflection on the constitution of human nature. We may respect these factors; indeed in our situation they are indispensable; but the whence and the whither, the power of faith and love on which tolerance rests for its fulfillment, cannot look to these quarters. Tolerance has to do in every period with the new and the living, the work of the Spirit, to which many witnesses in history bear testimony, some weak, some strong, some clear, some obscure—and among them the document with which we have presently been occupied, the Edict of Toleration of the Emperor Constantine.

# Bibliographical Note

THERE IS an admirable introduction to the problems of
Constantinian research by Joseph Vogt in his article
"Constantine" in *Reallexikon für Antike und Christentum*,
t. 3 (1956), cols. 306–79, together with an excellent bib-
liography; cf. his essay "Das römische Weltreich im Zeitalter Konstantins des Grossen-Wirklichkeit und Idee,
Saeculum," 9 (1958), 308–21. The documents are dis-
cussed in my *Das Selbstzeugnis Kaiser Konstantins*, Göttingen, 1954. My own appraisal of Constantine's work
is given in my *Konstantin der Grosse*, Stuttgart, 1958.

Literature on Diocletian: W. Seston, *Dioclétien et la
Tétrarchie, t.* 1 (Paris, 1946), and the same in *Reallexikon
für Antike und Christentum*, 3 (1956), cols. 1036–53.
With regard to the persecutions of the Christians, cf.
J. Vogt "Christenverfolgung, I," *Reallexicon für Antike
und Christentum*, 2 (1954), cols. 1159–1208, and J. Moreau, *La Persécution du Christianisme dans l'Empire Romain* (Paris, 1956); the most glaring exposition of the
opposite view: Henri Grégoire, *Les Persécutions dans
l'Empire Romain* (Brussels, 1951), with which cf. the
review of H. von Campenhausen, *Gnomon, 25* (1953),
464–67.

From the extensive literature on religious liberty the following may be mentioned: Miner Searle Bates, *Religious*

133

*Liberty: An Inquiry* (New York, 1945), an appraisal of the contemporary scene; N. G. Wood, *Religious Liberty Today* (Cambridge, 1949), a survey; E. C. Dewick, *The Christian Attitude to Other Religions* (Cambridge, 1953), an interpretation. For historical periods consult the following: Simeon L. Guterman, *Religious Toleration and Persecution in Ancient Rome*, London, 1951; Joseph Lecler, S.J., *Histoire de la tolérance au siècle de la reforme*, 2 vols. Paris, 1955; Johannes Kuehn, *Toleranz und Offenbarung*, Leipzig, 1923; W. K. Jordan, *The Development of Religious Toleration in England*, 4 vols. Cambridge, Mass., 1932–46; Thomas Lyon, *The Theory of Religious Liberty in England, 1603–39*, Cambridge, England, 1939; Michael Freund, "Die Idee der Toleranz in England . . ." *Deutsche Viertel-Jahrschrift für Literaturwissenschaft und Geistesgeschichte*, Buchreihe, *t. 12*, Halle, 1927; Roland H. Bainton, *Castellio Concerning Heretics*, New York, 1935; Bainton, *The Travail of Religious Liberty*, Philadelphia, 1951.

# Index

136

Instinsky, U., 86 n.
Isis, cult of, in Rome, 5

Jerome, St., 104
Jews: exempted from complying with imperial cult, 6; ransomed Hitler prisoners, 71
Julian, 101 n.; repudiated Constantine's policy, 50–51
Justinian, 52

Knipfing, John R., opinion of Galerius' edict of A.D. *311*, 15 n.

Lactantius, 10 n., 22 n.; free will necessary to religion, 4
Lenin, 77
Libanius, 53, 63, 64
Licinius, 24, 37; issues Edict of Milan, 17–19; victor over Maximinus Daza, 19; role of Constantine and, in formulation of Edict, 19–20 n.; a sun worshiper, 20 n., 23; Constantine's war against, 25; oppression of Christians, 41
Lord's Supper, 84; adopted into pagan cult, 51
Luther, Martin, 129–30, 130 n.

Manichees: Diocletian's Edict against, 10–11; harsh treatment of, 11
Marcionites, 111
Martyrs, "church" of. *See* Meletians
Maximian, Sabinus-Rescript, 23 n.
Maximinus Daza, 19; edicts of, 24
Medieval Church, 56, 59
Meletians, 116, 117
Milan, Edict of, 17–23, 28, 31, 32, 39, 41, 42, 92; issued, 17–19; interpreted (origin, aim, and presuppositions), 20 ff.; compared with edict of Galerius, 21–22
Mill, John Stuart, on liberty, 72 n.
Milvian Bridge, Battle of, 17, 19 n.
Moreau, J., 22–23 n.

Nicaea, Council of, 30 n., 93–95, 109, 110, 112–14, 116, 118, 119, 121–23

Nicene doctrine, 117

Nikomedia, 22 n.

Northern Africa, schismatic church of, 57. *See also* African Church

Novatianists, 111, 113, 117

Numidian bishops, in Donatist controversy at Carthage, 83

Origen, promised spiritual support to imperial forces, 2

Ossius, Bishop of Cordova, 88

Paul, Apostle, 59

Paulicians, 111

Persecution of Christians, 6, 7, 12–13; inevitability of, 13–14; Galerius chief instigator, 15

Persian Kingdom, 42–43

Peter, Apostle, 51

Phrygians, 111

Pliny the younger, letter to Trajan, 7–8

Porphyry, 120, 121

Ranke, Leopold, 65

Ransom, paid for religious leaders, down to Hitler era, 70–71 n.

Religion: of Tertullian, 2–3; a matter of inner persuasion, 3–4, 26, 30, 57; free will necessary to, 4, 26, 30, 57. *See also under names of Churches*

Roman Church, two famous examples showing policy of, 7–12. *See also* Emperor worship

Roman empire: Christian arguments for freedom in, before Constantine, 1–3; allowed conquered peoples to retain religion, 5–6; compliance with imperial cult a condition for toleration of alien religion, 6; the deed of worshiping important, not the word, 6; never relinquished religious foundations, 8–9; desire to maintain a religious interpretation, 11. *See also* Roman religion

Roman religion, core of, 7. *See also* Roman church, Roman empire

Ruffini, Francesco, 72–73 n.

Sacrifice, not to be forced, 3
Schapur II, 42, 43
Symmachus, 53
Syrians: cult of sun god in Rome, 5; allowed own religion, 5

Tertullian, 30; grounds religion in personal conviction, 2–3
Theodosius, 50 n., 56, 64, 81, 125; decree of A.D. *380*, 51–52;
    intolerance of church of, 54; model for Augustine, 61
Theodosius II, *Codex*, 52, 120
Theognis, 118
Tolerance: Pre-Constantinian plea for, 1–5; of Romans, based
    on two facts, 6; intolerance of Pre-Constantinian Romans,
    6; religious nonessentials the core of Roman, 7; Roman
    intolerance was directed against cultus, not teaching, 8;
    province of the mighty, 14; defined, 14 n., 75 and n., 76–77;
    renewed after Constantine's war against Licinius, 26; height-
    ened duty of, laid upon Christians, 29; extended to Persian
    treatment of Romans, 43; parallels with Constantine's, 48–
    49 n.; Christian vs. pagan intolerance, 54–55; intolerance
    sharpened by Christian rulers of Rome, 55–56; demanded
    by truth, 66; Constantine in the light of modern, 67 ff.;
    three questions addressed to Constantine in light of modern,
    77–78. *See also* Toleration
Toleration: defined, 14 n.; two stages of, 42
Toleration, Edicts of: A.D. *311*, 16–17, 21, 23, 24, 41; A.D. *324*,
    39–40, 41, 63, 131
Trajan, pattern of good emperors, 8
Tyre: inscription preserved at, 25; Synod of, 92 n., 121

Valentinians, 111
Valerian, 42 n.
Venus, closing of temples of, 45
Voltaire, 49 n.

Western Church, 56, 88
Worship, cannot be forced, 4, 26, 30, 57

Zurich, Reformed Church of, 52

important bearing on the subject, all the great laws of nature, especially of evolution . . . also such interpretations of literature and sociology as are in accord with the spirit of this Foundation, to the end that the Christian spirit may be nurtured in the fullest light of the world's knowledge and that mankind may be helped to attain its highest possible welfare and happiness upon this earth . . .

"The lectures shall be subject to no philosophical and religious test and no one who is an earnest seeker after truth shall be excluded because his views seem radical or destructive of existing beliefs. The founder realizes that the liberalism of one generation is often conservatism in the next, and that many an apostle of true liberty has suffered martyrdom at the hands of the orthodox. He therefore lays special emphasis on complete freedom of utterance, and would welcome expressions of conviction from sincere thinkers of differing standpoints even when these may run counter to the generally accepted views of the day. The founder stipulates only that the managers of the fund shall be satisfied that the lecturers are well qualified for their work and are in harmony with the cardinal principles of the Foundation, which are loyalty to the truth, lead where it will, and devotion to human welfare."

Volumes Published by the Yale University Press
on the Dwight Harrington Terry Foundation